Say it Better in English

*Useful Phrases for Work &
Everyday Life*

Marianna Pascal

ANN ARBOR, MICHIGAN

First Edition
Printed in the United States of America

ISBN 10: 0-9725300-8-8
ISBN 13: 978-0-9725300-8-8

Library of Congress Control Number: 2007926534

Visit our website: www.languagesuccesspress.com
For free English exercises and more, visit: www.eslmania.com

Bulk discounts are available. For information, please contact:

Language Success Press
2232 S. Main Street #345
Ann Arbor, MI 48103
USA

E-mail: sales@languagesuccesspress.com
Fax: (303) 484-2004 (USA)

To my father, Harold Pascal

About the Author

Marianna Pascal has taught English as a Second Language in Canada, the United States, Australia, and Southeast Asia. She currently operates her own language school in Malaysia.

In addition to teaching, Marianna, from Montreal, Canada, has developed English language course material for Excel Books and Scholani Educational College in Australia, for ELS Language Centers in Malaysia, and for her own school.

Married to a Chinese Malaysian, Marianna has been a presenter at several international language conferences and has published papers on language teaching in educational journals.

About the Illustrator

Lee Shee earned a degree in Fine Arts from the National Taiwan Normal University. She is a freelance illustrator and has illustrated projects from greeting cards to books to product packaging. For more of Lee Shee's illustrations, visit www.leesheeart.com.

HOW TO USE THIS BOOK

Dear Reader,

We know that you are busy. You want to learn fast. This book was designed to make it easy for you. You can use the book these ways:

1. **Read it like a storybook**
   Say it Better in English tells the story of five people who work together.

2. **Learn one phrase a day**
   We suggest you read one page each day from Monday to Saturday.

Puzzle review
After every six pages, see how much you have learned by doing the crossword puzzle.

When you do a puzzle, pay attention to the verb tense. For example, you may have to write 'made' instead of 'make'.

Examples
See each phrase used in more everyday situations.

At the bottom of some pages, you are asked to see another page. This helps you to understand a phrase in the example. You will see some phrases many times. This will help you to remember them.

Take the phrases with you

If you want to carry the phrases with you to practice wherever you go, you can print out a free list of all these phrases and their meanings. You'll find this tool on the Language Success Press website: www.languagesuccesspress.com.

See it, then say it

When you learn a phrase, try to use it the same day.

Enjoy!

- Marianna Pascal

keep going

continue

MORE EXAMPLES 🗨

A: "Can I stop running?"
B: "No, **keep going**. You need the exercise."

A: "Should we stop working at 6 o'clock?"
B: "No, let's **keep going** until 8 o'clock."

Mr. Lee

NOT ~~Mr. Alan~~

MORE EXAMPLES 🗨

A: "I'm Bill Jones."
B: "Nice to meet you, **Mr.** Jones."
A: "You can call me by my first name."
B: "Alright. Hello Bill."

A: "I'd like you to meet Don Clinton."
B: "Hello **Mr.** Clinton."

drop by

visit for a short time

MORE EXAMPLES 🗩

"You left your book in my car. I'll **drop by** your house and give it to you."

"I **dropped by** the camera store to pick up our photos."

For *left*, see page 232
For *pick up*, see page 62

Can I put you on hold?

Please wait.

Ask this during a phone call.

MORE EXAMPLES 🗨

A: "Can I speak to the manager?"
B: "**Can I put you on hold** for a minute? I'll see if he's here."

A: "Hello, ABC Market? Do you have any fresh raspberries?"
B: "**Can I put you on hold** while I go and see if we have any left?"

For *left*, see page 185

in charge of

responsible for; supervisor of

MORE EXAMPLES 🖝

"I'd like to speak to the person **in charge of** customer service."

"He's **in charge of** train**ing** new staff."

NOTE: sometimes **in charge of** + _ing

running short of time

getting close to a deadline

MORE EXAMPLES 🗩

"I have to work late tonight. I need to finish a project, and I'm **running short of time**."

"I'd like to finish this meeting soon. Let's move on to the next point because we're **running short of time**."

For *move on*, see page 209

Grab a Pencil! · Puzzle #1

ACROSS

1) "This is Stephen Jackson." ▪ "Nice to meet you, Mr. ___."

4) "Your test is tomorrow. You haven't studied yet! You're running ___ ___ time!"

5) "Let's stop driving and have dinner." ▪ "No, let's ___ ___. We will be there soon."

6) (on the phone) "What time is the meeting?" ▪ "Can I put you ___ ___? I'll ask my boss."

DOWN

2) "I'm a teacher. I'm in ___ ___ 50 students."

3) "If you ___ ___ my house tonight, I'll give you the money."

For answers, see page 365

get a move on

go faster

MORE EXAMPLES 🗩

"The movie is going to start soon. Let's **get a move on** or we'll be late."

"We have to **get a move on** if we want to finish by Wednesday."

For *by Wednesday*, see page 117

that's K for Korea

Say this to help people understand
the spelling of a word.

MORE EXAMPLES 🗩

A: "What's your email address?"
B: "It's alan76@hotmail.com. **That's** A **for** Africa, L **for** London, A **for** Africa, N **for** Norway, the number 76, at hotmail dot com."

A: "My address is 22 Elm Street."
B: "Sorry, what street?"
A: "Elm. **That's** E **for** England, L **for** London, M **for** Mexico."

How can I help you?

This is often used when answering
the phone in a workplace.

MORE EXAMPLES 💬

"Good afternoon. ABC Marketing. **How can
I help you?**"

"IMG Computers. This is Mary speaking.
How can I help you?"

it's for you

the caller wants to speak to you

MORE EXAMPLES 🗩

"Could you ask Chris to come to the phone? **It's for** him. It's his mother."

A: "The phone is ringing."
B: "I'll get it. I think **it's for** me."

For *I'll get it*, see page 61

in an hour

one hour **after now**

NOT ~~an hour later~~; NOT ~~after an hour~~

MORE EXAMPLES 🗨

"She hasn't arrived yet. She'll be here **in** 10 minutes."

"He is almost finished with high school. He will graduate **in** a few months."

For a different meaning of *in*, see page 215

ahead of / on / behind schedule

faster than planned / as planned / slower than planned

MORE EXAMPLES 💬

"Please drive faster. We are **behind schedule**."

A: "How's the project coming along?"
B: "Fine. Everything is **on schedule**."

For *coming along*, see page 228

Grab a Pencil! ▪ Puzzle #2

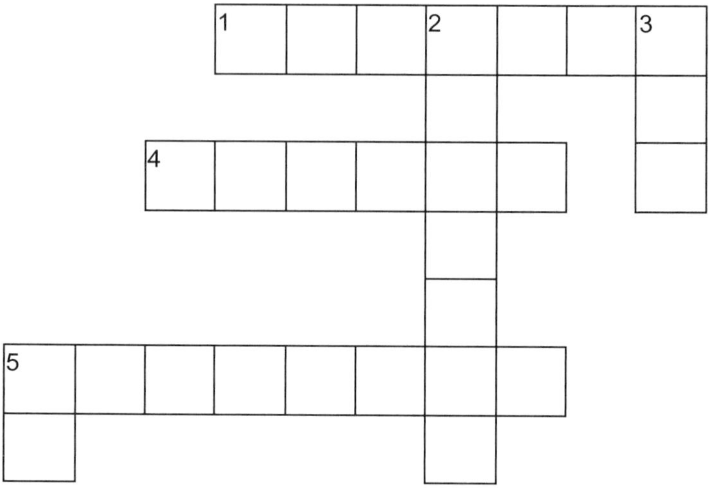

<u>ACROSS</u>

1) "Don't forget to finish the report tomorrow."
   ▪ "I've already finished. I'm ___ ___ schedule."
4) (on the phone) "Can I speak to Jane?" ▪ "One moment, please.... Jane! ___ ___ you."
5) (on the phone) "Good afternoon. This is the Hinton Hotel. How can ___ ___ ___?"

<u>DOWN</u>

2) "Hurry up! We have to get ___ ___ ___."
   ▪ "Okay. I'll get my coat quickly."
3) "My name is Sam. That's S ___ Sweden, A, M."
5) "I am driving to work now. I will arrive at work ___ 15 minutes."

For answers, see page 365

tied up

busy doing something that you can't stop

MORE EXAMPLES 💬

A: "Can we meet today?"
B: "Sorry, I'll be **tied up** all day. How about tomorrow?"

"I'm **tied up** now, but I'll be free in an hour."

For *in an hour*, see page 12

When is a good time?

When is a convenient time for you?

MORE EXAMPLES

"I have some papers for you to sign. **When is a good time** to drop by your office?"

A: "Can we meet next week?"
B: "Sure. **When is a good time** for you?"
A: "How about Friday at 10 a.m.?"

For *drop by*, see page 3

held up

delayed

MORE EXAMPLES 🗩

"I was **held up** at the airport for two hours! Customs officials went through my bags."

"I got home at 10 o'clock last night. I was **held up** at the office doing paperwork."

NOTE: paperwork = work that involves forms, documents and letters

For *went through*, see page 194

move something
out of the way

move something **so that it doesn't block you**

Please move these boxes out of the way!

MORE EXAMPLES 🗨

"We're having a party, so I want to **move** the furniture **out of the way**."

"There are a lot of things on your desk. If you **move** them **out of the way**, I'll put your computer there."

upside down / right side up

with the top part at the bottom / with the top part at the top

MORE EXAMPLES 🗩

"Look! That picture is **upside down**. You hung it the wrong way."

"There's a cake in this box. Please make sure the box is **right side up**."

For *make sure*, see page 353

no wonder

now I understand why

MORE EXAMPLES 🗩

A: "Why is he so sad?"
B: "His wife just died."
A: "**No wonder** he's sad."

A: "This lamp doesn't work."
B: "You didn't plug it in!"
A: "**No wonder** it doesn't work!"

For *plug it in*, see page 124
For *doesn't work*, see page 162

Grab a Pencil! · Puzzle #3

ACROSS

3) "Please move your bicycle ___ ___ the way so I can park here."

5) "I need to talk to you, but I know you are busy. When is a ___ ___?" ▪ "How about 4 o'clock?"

6) "Sorry I'm late. I was ___ ___ at the post office. There was a long line!"

DOWN

1) "Why are you so tired?" ▪ "I just ran 15 miles." ▪ "Wow! ___ ___ you're tired!"

2) If the number 6 is ___ ___, it looks like the number 9.

4) "Can you help me?" ▪ "Sorry, I'm ___ ___ right now. I'm helping another customer."

For answers, see page 365

on me

Say this if you want to pay for
someone's food or drink.

MORE EXAMPLES 🗩

A: "Lunch is **on me** today."
B: "Thanks Jack."
A: "It's my pleasure."

A: "Let's split the check."
B: "No, the drinks are **on me** today."

For *split the check,* see page 183

stuck in traffic

in a traffic jam

Sue, I'll be home late. I'm stuck in traffic.

MORE EXAMPLES 🗩

"Sorry I'm late. I was **stuck in traffic** for an hour."

"There's no point in driving downtown during rush hour. You'll be **stuck in traffic**."

NOTE: rush hour = the times of day with the busiest traffic, when many people are traveling to or from work

For *there's no point,* see page 212

it slipped my mind

I forgot

MORE EXAMPLES 🗩

A: "Did you mail my letter?"
B: "Oh, **it slipped my mind**. I'll do it tomorrow."

"I was supposed to meet Fred last night, but
I forgot. **It slipped my mind**."

For *supposed to*, see page 305

under a lot of pressure

feeling stress

MORE EXAMPLES 💬

"We are **under a lot of pressure** because we have to finish this job by Friday."

"Students are **under a lot of pressure** at exam time."

For *by Friday*, see page 117

drop something **off**

take something to a place and leave it there

MORE EXAMPLES 🗩

"I'm going to the dry cleaners. I want to **drop off** some shirts."

A: "Don't stay and talk. Just **drop off** the gift and leave."
B: "Okay, I'll just **drop** it **off**."

NOTE: **drop** something **off**, **drop off** something, **drop** it **off**, NOT ~~drop off it~~

Have you done something **yet?**

Ask this to find out if something has *already* happened.

MORE EXAMPLES 🗨

A: "**Have you** eaten lunch **yet**?"
B: "Yes, I had lunch an hour ago."

A: "**Have you** been to the post office **yet**?"
B: "No, not yet. I'm going now."

For *ago*, see page 46

Grab a Pencil! ▪ Puzzle #4

			1				
2					3		
	4						
	5						

ACROSS

2) (at a restaurant) "I'll pay." ▪ "No, lunch is ___ ___ this time." ▪ "Thank you."

4) "Why are you late?" ▪ "I was ___ ___ traffic."

5) "Have you had lunch ___?" ▪ "No, I'm hungry."

DOWN

1) "I have a lot of deadlines this month. I'm under a lot of ___."

2) "Could you take this book back to the library?" ▪ "Yes, I'll drop it ___ on my way to work."

3) "You forgot to buy milk!" ▪ "Sorry. I was so busy it slipped ___ ___."

For answers, see page 365

get through

make contact with someone **by phone**

MORE EXAMPLES 🗩

A: "I tried to call you, but I couldn't **get through**."

B: "Sorry. I turned off my cell phone."

"Don't call the bank at lunchtime. They are so busy. It's difficult to **get through**."

For *it's difficult to*, see page 300

put up with something

accept something bad

MORE EXAMPLES 🗪

"Your neighbor's dog is so noisy! How can you **put up with** the noise?"

"My office is freezing, but I **put up with** it because I love my job."

NOTE: freezing = very cold

right away

immediately; now

MORE EXAMPLES 🗩

A: "Waiter! I ordered soup 30 minutes ago!"
B: "I'm sorry, Sir. I'll bring it **right away**."

A: "The client is waiting. He needs the report."
B: "I'll get it **right away**."

For *ago*, see page 46

x **caused** y / y **was caused by** x

x **made** y **happen** / y **happened because of** x

MORE EXAMPLES 🖙

A: "What **caused** the delay?"
B: "Heavy rain **caused** the delay."

A: "The goods are damaged!"
B: "The damage **was caused by** the shipping department."

it's not the end of the world

the situation is not very bad

It's not the end of the world. Your hair will grow back.

MORE EXAMPLES 🗩

"I hurt my knee, but **it's not the end of the world**. I can still play golf."

A: "I failed my driving test!"
B: "**It's not the end of the world**. You can take the test again."

in the same boat

in the same bad situation

MORE EXAMPLES 🖝

A: "My husband is often away on business."
B: "So is mine! We're **in the same boat**."

"We all lost money last year. We're all **in the same boat**."

For *away on business,* see page 262

ACROSS
4) "I called Fred 10 times, but I can't ___ ___. The line is always busy."
5) "I lost your report!" ▪ "Don't worry. It's not the end of ___ ___. I can print another copy."
6) "What caused the car accident?" ▪ "The accident ___ caused ___ ice on the road."

DOWN
1) "I lost my job this year." ▪ "I lost my job too! We are in the same ___."
2) "Joe is sick. Call the doctor!" ▪ "Let's wait." ▪ "No, don't wait! Call him ___ ___!"
3) "My wife talks too much! She'll never change, so I ___ ___ with her talking."

For answers, see page 365

I'm not following you

Say this if you don't understand instructions, directions or an explanation.

MORE EXAMPLES

A: "To save the document, click on 'copy' then open a new file and click..."
B: "**I'm not following you**. Click on what?"

A: "He's not unfriendly, he's just not friendly."
B: "**I'm not following you**."

get cut off

lose the connection during a telephone call

MORE EXAMPLES 🗩

"There's something wrong with my phone. I often **get cut off**."

A: "Hello?"
B: "Hi. This is John again. We **got cut off** just now, so I'm calling you back."

For *there's something wrong with*, see page 347
For *call you back*, see page 193

have change

have smaller units of money

MORE EXAMPLES 🗩

A: "Do you **have change** for $10?"
B: "Yes, here are nine ones and some small change."

A: "Your coffee is $3, please."
B: "Here's a 50 dollar bill."
A: "Sorry. I don't **have change** for a fifty."

NOTE: small change = coins; bill = paper money; a fifty = a fifty dollar bill

distance **from** a place

Say this to show the distance between two places.

MORE EXAMPLES 🗩

A: "Where's Palo Alto?"
B: "It's about 30 miles **from** San Francisco."

"Our office is about 200 feet **from** Grand Central Station."

the second to last

the thing before the last thing

Mr. Franks can see you now. It's the second to last door: the black door.

MORE EXAMPLES 🗩

"We went to France for a week. We were having a great time. But on **the second to last** day, I got sick."

A: "Which is your house?"
B: "**The second to last** house on the street."

comes in

is available in

MORE EXAMPLES 🖝

"This phone **comes in** blue, white or black. Which one should I buy?"

"Instant soup **comes in** a plastic cup. And it **comes in** two flavors: chicken and beef. I prefer the beef soup."

For *prefer*, see page 247

GRAB A PENCIL! · Puzzle #6

ACROSS

2) (on a cell phone) "Speak quickly. My battery is low. We might get ___ ___."
4) "Was Joe the last person to arrive?" ▪ "Almost. He was the ___ ___ last person."
5) "This jacket ___ ___ three sizes: small, medium and large."
6) "I need 25 cents for the phone, but I only have a $10 bill. Do you ___ ___?"

DOWN

1) "Turn left, turn right, then right again, then left..." ▪ "Huh? I'm not ___ you. Could you start over?"
3) "Do you live near your office?" ▪ "Yes, I live just two miles ___ my office."

For answers, see page 365

I'd like

This is a polite way to say what you want.

NOT ~~I want~~

MORE EXAMPLES 💬

A: "**I'd like** a ticket to Stanton City, please."
B: "One-way or a round-trip ticket?"

A: "Can I help you?"
B: "Yes, **I'd like** to send this package to Mexico City."

NOTE: a round-trip ticket = a ticket that takes you somewhere, then brings you back

I've been waiting for a long time

Say this for something you are still doing now.

MORE EXAMPLES 💬

"I hope we arrive soon. We've been sitting in this airplane for seven hours!"

"Please wake up the baby. He's been sleeping for four hours."

NOTE: I've = I have; we've = we have; he's = he has

make up my mind

decide

MORE EXAMPLES 💬

A: "Are you going to buy the blue car or the green car?"

B: "I don't know. I haven't **made up** my **mind** yet."

"He's finally **made up** his **mind**. He's going to study business."

two weeks **ago**

two weeks **before now**

MORE EXAMPLES

A: "I just got married."
B: "When?"
A: "Three days **ago**."

"He left the office five minutes **ago**. You just missed him."

cheers

Sometimes we say this before drinking alcohol to offer good wishes.

When we say this, we lift our glasses and touch them together.

Cheers!

MORE EXAMPLES 🗩

A: "**Cheers**!"
B: "**Cheers**! To a long happy life."

A: "**Cheers**. To your health."
B: "**Cheers**."

For *to*, see page 101

discuss something

talk about something

NOT ~~discuss about something~~

MORE EXAMPLES

"We need to **discuss the travel arrangements**."

"We can **discuss the situation** at the meeting if you bring it up."

For *bring it up*, see page 178

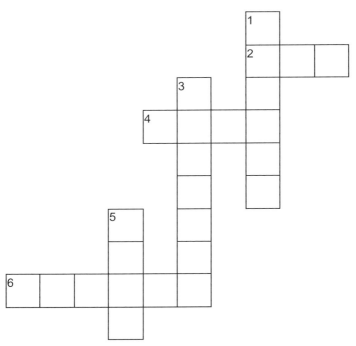

ACROSS

2) "We bought this house 25 years ___."

4) "Can I help you, Sir?" ▪ "Yes, I'd ___ two coffees, please."

6) Rearrange these letters to make a word that we sometimes say before drinking alcohol: ceresh

DOWN

1) "Do you want to order the chicken or the fish?" ▪ "I don't know. I can't ___ ___ my mind."

3) "When can we talk about the computer problem?" ▪ "We can ___ it now."

5) "I'm studying now. I'm tired because I've ___ studying for three hours!"

For answers, see page 365

stay up

stay awake later than one's usual bedtime

You go to sleep.
I'm going to stay up.

MORE EXAMPLES 🖤

A: "Why are you so tired today?"
B: "I **stayed up** late last night."

"When my husband works late, I **stay up**
until he gets home."

oversleep

wake up later than planned

MORE EXAMPLES 🗩

"I'm behind schedule this morning because I **overslept**."

"I use three alarm clocks so that I never **oversleep**."

For *behind schedule,* see page 13

about to do something

going to do something *very* soon

MORE EXAMPLES 🗩

A: "Is Dan still here?"
B: "Yes, but you'd better talk to him now.
   He's **about to** leave."

A: "Have you written that letter yet?"
B: "No, but I'm **about to** do it right now."

For *Have you ... yet?*, see page 27

on my way

going to a place — but not at the place yet

MORE EXAMPLES 🗩

A: "Did you call the police?"
B: "Yes, they're **on** their **way**. They will be here very soon."

A: "We need some milk."
B: "Okay, I'll ask Dad to buy some **on** his **way** home."

get sidetracked

become distracted from something important

MORE EXAMPLES 🗩

A: "You burned dinner."
B: "Yes. While I was cooking, my mom called and I **got sidetracked**."

"I didn't finish my homework. There was a good movie on TV, so I **got sidetracked**."

gone for the day

Say this when someone will *not* come back that day.

Do you know where Mr. Lee is?

He's gone for the day.

MORE EXAMPLES 🗩

A: "Could I speak to Mr. Couga?"
B: "Sorry, he's **gone for the day**. He will be in the office tomorrow morning."

"Kate's **gone for the day**. You can reach her at home."

For *reach*, see page 254

GRAB A PENCIL! · Puzzle #8

ACROSS

5) "Are you busy?" ▪ "Yes. I just finished cooking dinner, and I am about ___ eat it."

6) "I was busy working. Then my friend visited me, and I forgot about work. I got ___."

DOWN

1) "If I don't set my alarm clock at night, I will ___ in the morning."

2) "Last night I didn't go to bed early. I ___ ___ until 2 a.m."

3) "My assistant is gone ___ ___ day. She'll be back in the office tomorrow."

4) "I'm in my car driving to my office. I'm on ___ ___ to work."

For answers, see page 365

in the lighting **business**

Say this to show the industry someone works in.

That's Mr. Lee.
He's in the
lighting business.

MORE EXAMPLES 🗩

"Mr. Saito is **in the** shoe **business**. He exports shoes."

A: "What do you do?"
B: "I'm **in the** publishing **business**. I'm an editor."

NOTE: What do you do? = What is your job?

a win-win situation

a situation that has good results
in many ways

MORE EXAMPLES 🗩

"Buying a house is **a win-win situation**. If you sell it, you make money. If you keep it, you make money."

"I rent a room in my brother's house. He needs the extra money. I need a room. It's **a win-win situation**."

that's it

nothing more

MORE EXAMPLES 🗩

A: "You're going to Europe? To France? Germany? Spain?"
B: "Just to Italy. **That's it**."

A: "We have just 24 hours to finish this project!"
B: "Twenty four hours? **That's it**?"
A: "Yes, that's all the time we have."

it's about time

it is overdue, but it is finally happening

MORE EXAMPLES 🗩

A: "The package arrived."
B: "**It's about time**! I've been waiting for weeks!"

A: "Sam is getting married."
B: "Great. **It's about time**. He's 46 years old."

For *I've been waiting*, see page 44

get it

answer the phone

MORE EXAMPLES 🗩

A: "The phone's ringing."
B: "I'll **get it**. I think it's for me."

A: "The phone's ringing."
B: "Could you **get it**? I'm busy."

For *it's for me,* see page 11

pick something **up**

collect something

MORE EXAMPLES 🗩

"I left my book at your house. Could I come over later and **pick** it **up**?"

A: "I'm from ABC Company. I'm here to **pick up** an envelope."
B: "Oh, yes, here it is."

NOTE: **pick** something **up**, **pick up** something, **pick** it **up**, NOT pick up it

For *left*, see page 232

ACROSS

2) "This situation is good for you and good for me. It's a ___-___ situation."

5) "For lunch I eat an apple." ▪ "Just an apple?" ▪ "Yes, that's ___. I'm on a diet."

6) "The phone is ringing." ▪ "I'm in the shower!" ▪ "Okay. I'll ___ ___."

DOWN

1) "Yesterday, I took my shirt to the cleaners. When it's clean, I'll ___ it ___."

3) "What business are you in?" ▪ "I'm ___ ___ furniture business. I import furniture from China."

4) "Mary finally graduated from college." ▪ "It's ___ time! She's been studying for 10 years!"

For answers, see page 365

Can I take a rain check?

Can we change the plan to another time in the future?

MORE EXAMPLES 🗨

A: "I have to cancel our plans for lunch today. **Can I take a rain check?**"
B: "Sure. How about tomorrow?"

A: "Would you like to go out for dinner tonight?"
B: "Sorry, I can't make it tonight. **Can I take a rain check?**"

For *can't make it*, see page 352

take time **off**

decide not to go to work for a short time

MORE EXAMPLES 💬

"I **took** three months **off** after I had the baby."

"I'm going to **take** a week **off** because I need a vacation."

on top of that

in addition to; also

Say this when the last piece of information is important.

MORE EXAMPLES

"My neighbor is noisy. He plays loud music at night and he has lots of parties. **On top of that**, his dog barks a lot!"

"I'm very busy. I have two children, I work full-time, and **on top of that** I take evening classes."

put clothes **on**

This is not the same as 'wear' clothes: first we **put** clothes **on**; *then* we are wearing clothes.

MORE EXAMPLES 🗩

"I ate breakfast quickly, **put** my coat **on** and ran out of the house."

"He's only two years old. He doesn't know how to **put on** his shoes."

NOTE: **put** something **on**, **put on** something, **put** it **on**, NOT ~~put on it~~

For *doesn't know how*, see page 331

I didn't mean that

Say this when someone does not
understand what you said.

NOT ~~That's not my meaning~~

MORE EXAMPLES 💬

A: "You're very big."
B: "You think I'm fat!"
A: "No, **I didn't mean that**. I meant you're
very tall."

A: "I want you to work over the weekend."
B: "Boss, I can't work *every* weekend!"
A: "**I didn't mean that**. I meant *this* week-
end."

Do you mind if I join you?

Ask this for permission to be with someone.

MORE EXAMPLES 🗨

A: "We're going to the movies."
B: "**Do you mind if I join you?**"
A: "No, we don't mind. Please come along."

A: "Hi Jane. **Do you mind if I join you?**"
B: "Actually, I'm leaving now, but you can have my seat."

ACROSS
1) "I broke my leg! I can't go to work, so I'm taking two weeks ___."
2) "I'm going out to lunch." ▪ "Do you ___ ___ I join you?" ▪ "No. Please come."
3) "I can't meet you for lunch today. Can I take a rain ___?"
4) "Firefighters have to wake up and ___ ___ their clothes very fast."

DOWN
1) "My girlfriend is smart, interesting and sweet. On top ___ ___, she's beautiful."
2) "These shoes cost nine ninety." ▪ "$990!" ▪ "No, I didn't ___ that. I meant $9.90."

For answers, see page 365

chip in

contribute money

MORE EXAMPLES 🗨

"Every summer, my friends and I **chip in** $100 each to rent a boat."

"My older brothers and sisters **chipped in** to pay for my education."

drop someone **off**

take someone **to a place and leave them there**

MORE EXAMPLES ✎

A: "Could you **drop** me **off** at the bank?"
B: "Sure, I'm going to drive right past the bank."

A: "Why are you late?"
B: "I **dropped** Sharon **off** at her house. Her car broke down."

What's the difference between A and B?

How are A and B different?

MORE EXAMPLES 🗩

A: "**What's the difference between** the words 'large' and 'big'?"

B: "There's no difference."

A: "**What's the difference between** these two cell phones?"

B: "One has a digital camera and the other one doesn't."

end up doing something

finally do something

MORE EXAMPLES 🗩

"Tim was a bad student. How did he **end up** becom**ing** a doctor?"

"At first business was good. But our costs were very high. So, we **ended up** los**ing** money."

you shouldn't have

Say this to show appreciation
when receiving a gift.

MORE EXAMPLES 💬

A: "I bought you this gift."
B: "Thank you, but **you shouldn't have**."
A: "It's nothing really."

A: "Happy Anniversary!"
B: "A gift for me? **You shouldn't have**!"
A: "My pleasure."

NOTE: "It's nothing" and "my pleasure" are
polite replies to "thank you".

75

the day after tomorrow

NOT ~~tomorrow after tomorrow~~

MORE EXAMPLES 🖅

"Tomorrow is July 3rd, so **the day after tomorrow** is July 4th."

A: "I'm getting married in three days!"
B: "So **the day after tomorrow** is your last day as a single man."

For *in three days*, see page 12

ACROSS

4) "First Sue was my girlfriend, then Mary, then Lucy. But I ended ___ marrying Jane."
5) "It's an overnight trip. We leave tomorrow and we return ___ ___ ___ tomorrow."
6) "Let's each ___ ___ five dollars and buy Fred a birthday present."

DOWN

1) "Every morning on my way to work, I ___ my son ___ at his school."
2) "What's the difference ___ a bicycle and a tricycle?" ▪ "A bicycle has two wheels; a tricycle has three."
3) "Happy Birthday! Here's a present." ▪ "Thank you, but you shouldn't ___!"

For answers, see page 365

take turns
do**ing** something

alternate (i.e. you, then me, then you, then me)

MORE EXAMPLES 🗩

"My partner and I **take turns** open**ing** the shop."

"Last year, my husband and I both worked, so we **took turns** cook**ing** dinner."

remind someone to

say something to help someone remember

MORE EXAMPLES 🗩

"Could you **remind** Sharon **to** order more envelopes? I think she forgot."

"When we get to the grocery store, please **remind** me **to** buy some eggs."

NOTE: grocery store = store that sells food and small household items

fed up with something

unhappy about something that has been happening for a long time

I'm fed up with the rain.

MORE EXAMPLES 🗩

"They're building a new house on my street. Every day they hammer and saw and drill! I'm **fed up with** all the noise."

"I don't like my job. I'm **fed up with** paperwork."

as long as

on the condition that; providing that

MORE EXAMPLES 💬

"We play football every Sunday morning **as long as** it's not raining."

A: "Boss, I'd like to leave at 4 o'clock today."
B: "That's fine **as long as** you finish the report first."

good at something

able to do something well

MORE EXAMPLES 🗩

"My father is very **good at** golf, but my mother isn't."

"Could you give me a hand with this letter? I'm not very **good at** writ**ing** in English."

NOTE: sometimes **good at** + **_ing**

For *give me a hand*, see page 176

so far, so good

**everything is fine *now*,
but there may be problems later on**

MORE EXAMPLES

A: "You fixed the printer again! How's it working?"
B: "**So far, so good**. I hope it doesn't break again."

A: "How's your new job?"
B: "I've only worked there for three days but **so far, so good**."

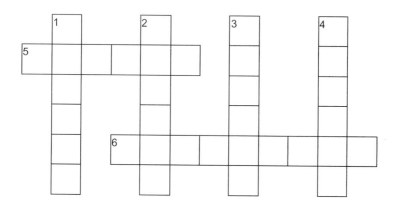

ACROSS

5) "I fixed my car." ▪ "Is it okay now?" ▪ "So far,
___ ___. But, it might break down again."

6) "Let's ___ ___ cleaning the house. You clean
on Mondays, and I'll clean on Thursdays."

DOWN

1) "Lisa is very ___ ___ math. She's the best in
her class."

2) "You can borrow my books as ___ ___ you return them when you finish."

3) "This summer is too hot! Every day it's hot!
I'm fed ___ ___ this weather."

4) "Please ___ Joe to buy milk." ▪ "Okay. Joe,
don't forget to buy milk!"

For answers, see page 365

that sounds

Say this to give your opinion after
reading or hearing something.

MORE EXAMPLES 🗨

A: "We stayed in a five-star hotel right on
the beach."

B: "**That sounds** beautiful."

A: "I'm going to climb up on the roof and fix
the leak."

B: "**That sounds** dangerous!"

you're not allowed to
do something
doing something **is not permitted**

Dad, you're not allowed to park here.

MORE EXAMPLES 🗩

"I read that **you're not allowed to** chew gum in Singapore."

"I can't work in the USA because I don't have a work permit. **You're not allowed to** work without a permit."

NOTE: In spoken English, "you" can mean "everyone".

despite something

not affected by something

MORE EXAMPLES 💬

"The company did well this year **despite** poor sales in March."

"He goes jogging every day **despite** hav**ing** a broken arm."

NOTE: sometimes **despite** + **_ing**

as a result

consequently; as an effect

MORE EXAMPLES 🗩

"My brother left school when he was 14. **As a result**, he can't find a good job."

"It rained a lot last year. **As a result**, we sold a lot of umbrellas."

Do you know where Mr. Smith **is?**

NOT ~~Do you know where is Mr. Smith?~~

MORE EXAMPLES 🔊

A: "**Do you know where** Ohio **is?**"
B: "I think it's near Pennsylvania."

A: "Terri, **do you know where** the July bank
   statement **is?**"
B: "I have no idea."

sorry to interrupt

Say this when you want to talk to someone who is already speaking.

MORE EXAMPLES 🖝

"**Sorry to interrupt**, but Mr. Marco wants to see you right now."

A: "Tuesday is a holiday so…"
B: "**Sorry to interrupt**, but *Wednesday* is a holiday, not Tuesday."
A: "Oh, yes. You're right."

GRAB A PENCIL! · Puzzle #13

ACROSS
1) "It rained all day, but we went swimming ___ the rain."
3) "Do you know ___ Bob ___?" ▪ "Yes, Bob is in the kitchen."
5) "You're ___ allowed ___ take a knife on an airplane."
6) "You didn't study for the test. ___ ___ result, you failed the test."

DOWN
2) "I'll tell you a story. Last week I went..."
   ▪ "___ ___ interrupt, but I have to go now."
4) "I'm reading a book about cars of the future."
   ▪ "That ___ interesting."

For answers, see page 365

in good condition / in perfect condition

not broken / like new

MORE EXAMPLES 🗨

"My car is **in perfect condition** because I take good care of it."

"Our house used to be in bad condition. We fixed everything, so now it's **in good condition**."

he **just stepped out**

he **went out for a short time**

MORE EXAMPLES 🖝

A: "Could I speak to Eva?"
B: "She **just stepped out** of the office. She'll be back soon."

A: "Fred's not in his office. Is he gone for the day?"
B: "No, he **just stepped out**."

For *back*, see page 264
For *gone for the day*, see page 55

I'll put you through

I will connect you

Say this during a phone call.

MORE EXAMPLES 🗨

A: "Could I speak to Mr. Lim?"
B: "He's not here right now. **I'll put you through** to his assistant."

A: "I'd like to speak to the manager."
B: "One moment, please. **I'll put you through**."

There's been a delay

Say this when something is late.

MORE EXAMPLES

A: "Has the package arrived yet?"
B: "No, **there's been a delay** because of bad weather."

"**There's been a delay** in production. One of the machines broke down."

for good

forever; permanently

MORE EXAMPLES 🍵

"There were ants in my kitchen. But after I used ant killer, they were gone **for good**!"

"I've tried to quit smoking before, but this time I'm quitting **for good**."

hear from someone

receive communication from someone

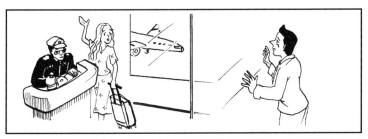

MORE EXAMPLES 🖝

A: "I **heard from** Jack last week. He emailed me."

B: "How is he?"

"I haven't **heard from** my sister for a long time. I hope she's okay."

ACROSS

3) "I heard ___ Sue. She emailed me last week. She's getting married."

5) "Sam just ___ ___ of the office for a few minutes.

6) "My bicycle is five years old, but it's ___ ___ condition because I take care of it."

DOWN

1) "Joe moved to Taiwan." ▪ "Is he coming back?" ▪ "No, he moved there for ___."

2) "Your shipment will arrive late because there's been ___ ___ at the customs department."

4) (on the phone) "Can I speak to the manager?" ▪ "Yes, I'll ___ ___ through to him."

For answers, see page 366

that's too bad

When someone tells you bad news,
say this to show that you care.

MORE EXAMPLES 🖝

A: "I didn't get the job."
B: "**That's too bad**. But I'm sure you'll get one soon."

A: "Our computer system has been down for five days!"
B: "**That's too bad**."

NOTE: down = not working

What's this charge for?

Ask this when you don't understand an amount on your bill or receipt.

MORE EXAMPLES 🗩

A: "**What's this charge for?**"
B: "That's the shipping charge."

A: "Excuse me. **What's this charge for** on my receipt?"
B: "It's the tax."

to someone / something

When people drink together, they say this to wish success to someone or something.

MORE EXAMPLES

(at a wedding) "**To** the bride and groom!"

(at a gathering of friends) "**To** friendship!"

(at a business dinner) "**To** our new partner-ship!"

I heard it through the grapevine

someone told me something as gossip or a rumor

Tom's wife is pregnant.

Tom's wife is pregnant.

Tom's wife is pregnant.

How did you know?

I heard it through the grapevine.

MORE EXAMPLES 🗩

A: "Alex lost his job."
B: "Who told you that?"
A: "**I heard it through the grapevine**."

A: "Are you sure the company is closing?"
B: "No, I'm not sure. **I heard it through the grapevine**."

hear back from someone

receive a reply from someone

MORE EXAMPLES 🗩

"I emailed Ted yesterday, and I hope to **hear back from** him soon."

A: "Did you get the job?"
B: "No. I had an interview, but I never **heard back from** the company."

really like / really enjoy / really want

NOT ~~very like~~ / NOT ~~very enjoy~~ / NOT ~~very want~~

MORE EXAMPLES 🗩

"Jane, I **really enjoyed** your presentation today."

"I **really like** my English class. I **really want** to improve my writing."

GRAB A PENCIL! · Puzzle #15

ACROSS
2) At a wedding, someone might lift their glass and say, "___ the bride and groom!"
3) "I wrote to her. I don't know if she got my letter because I didn't hear ___ from her."
5) "Do you like Italian food?" ▪ "Yes, I ___ like it! I like it a lot!"
6) "Todd got a new job! I heard it through the ___. Everyone is talking about it."

DOWN
1) "My mother is sick. She's in the hospital." ▪ "That's ___ ___."
4) "Waiter, what's this ___ for on my bill?" ▪ "That $4.59 on your bill is the tax."

For answers, see page 366

better off do**ing** something

Say this to show a better choice.

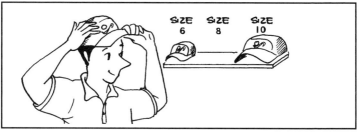

You're better off buying the size 8.

MORE EXAMPLES 🗩

A: "Should we go now?"
B: "No. There's too much traffic now. We're **better off** go**ing** later."

A: "The train takes three hours. The bus takes five hours."
B: "Then I'm **better off** tak**ing** the train."

the second one from the right / left

the thing *beside* the thing on the right / left

MORE EXAMPLES 🗩

"This is a photograph of my family. I'm **the second one from the right**."

"Please pass me that book on the shelf, **the second one from the left**."

Are we still on for today?

Are we going to meet as we have already agreed?

Ask this to confirm an arrangement.

MORE EXAMPLES

A: "**Are we still on for** tonight?"
B: "Yes. Let's meet at the theater at 7 p.m."

A: "**Are we still on for** lunch tomorrow?"
B: "Actually, I have to cancel. Can I take a rain check?"

For *Can I take a rain check*, see page 64

they say

some people say

Say this when you hear something,
but it's not important who said it.

They say it's going
to rain today.

MORE EXAMPLES 🗩

"**They say** it's important to get eight hours
of sleep a night."

A: "The economy is bad this year."
B: "Yes, but **they say** it will improve soon."

go ahead

do it

Say this if you want someone to start or do something.

MORE EXAMPLES 🖙

A: "Do you mind if I have the last cookie?"
B: "**Go ahead**. I've had enough."

A: "I'd like to start the meeting now."
B: "Okay, everyone's here, so **go ahead**."

in a good mood / in a bad mood

feeling happy / feeling unhappy

MORE EXAMPLES 🗨

A: "The boss looks angry."
B: "He's **in a bad mood** because sales are down this week."

A: "You're **in a good mood** today."
B: "Yes, I am. Tomorrow is a holiday!"

For *look angry*, see page 271

GRAB A PENCIL! · Puzzle #16

ACROSS

4) "In this photo, the man on the left is my father. Beside him is my mother. She's the ___ one ___ the left."

6) "Can I borrow your pen?" ▪ "Sure. Go ___. Take it."

DOWN

1) "You're smiling a lot today." ▪ "Yes, I'm ___ ___ ___ mood. I won $500!"

2) "Dinosaurs were very big." ▪ "Yes, ___ say that some were 30 feet tall!"

3) "I want to buy a dog, but my apartment is small." ▪ "Then you're better ___ buying a cat."

5) "Are we still ___ for dinner tonight?" ▪ "Yes. We're meeting at 7:30, right?"

For answers, see page 366

run into someone

meet someone unexpectedly

MORE EXAMPLES 💬

"I **ran into** Fred Schiffer at the airport. I was arriving from Seoul, and he was on his way to Chicago."

"Sometimes I **run into** Mohamed at the bank. We both go on Mondays."

For *on his way*, see page 53

I can't get something to work

I **can't make** something **function**

MORE EXAMPLES 🗩

"I've pressed all the buttons on this DVD player, but I **can't get** it **to work**."

"I **can't get** my printer **to work**. There's something wrong with it."

For *something wrong with it*, see page 347

take it apart /
put it back together

dismantle it / assemble it

MORE EXAMPLES 🗨

A: "What's wrong with the air conditioner?"
B: "I don't know. I'll **take** it **apart** and look inside."

"I took my computer apart to replace a part, and now I can't figure out how to **put** it **back together**."

For *can't figure out how to*, see page 160

this is Jenny

Say this to identify yourself on the phone.

NOT ~~I am Jenny~~

MORE EXAMPLES 🗩

A: "May I speak to the manager?"
B: "**This is** the manager speaking. How can I help you?"

A: "Can I speak to Mr. Daw?"
B: "Can I ask who's calling?"
A: "**This is** Mary from ABC Company."

For *How can I help you*, see page 10

by 9 o'clock

at 9:00 **or before** 9:00 —
but ***not* after** 9:00

MORE EXAMPLES 💬

"We need to be at the airport **by** 3 o'clock. Our flight leaves at 4 o'clock and we need one hour to check in."

"I need the report **by** 5 o'clock at the latest."

What do you think about do**ing** something?

NOT ~~How do you think about~~

MORE EXAMPLES 🍥

A: "**What do you think about** mov**ing** to a bigger house?"

B: "Good idea! We need more room."

A: "**What do you think about** buy**ing** a new car?"

B: "I don't think we need a new car."

GRAB A PENCIL! · Puzzle #17

ACROSS

2) "I took the wheels off my bike. Then I took the seat off." ▪ "Why did you take your bike ___?"

5) "What a boring party! People started to leave at 9 o'clock. ___ 9:30, everyone had gone."

6) "I ___ ___ your sister today! I was leaving Shopmart, and she was just coming in."

DOWN

1) "___ do you think ___ driving to the beach to-day?" ▪ "It's a great idea!"

3) (on the phone) "Hello Edward? ___ ___ Tony." ▪ "Hi Tony."

4) "Why don't you fix this broken radio?" ▪ "I've tried, but I can't get it to ___."

For answers, see page 366

we **don't see eye to eye**

This is a polite way to say we **don't agree**.

MORE EXAMPLES

"Steve loves the movie. Mary hates it. They **don't see eye to eye** on the movie."

"We both agree on the problem. But we **don't see eye to eye** on the solution."

on sale / for sale

cheaper than the regular price / available to buy

MORE EXAMPLES 🗩

"Hats are **on sale** at Shopmart this week. They are 20% off."

"Look! That house is **for sale**. I wonder how much it is."

NOTE: 20% off = 20% less than the normal price

What's something made of?

What materials were used to make something?

MORE EXAMPLES 🗩

A: "**What are** these shoes **made of**?"
B: "They're made of leather."

A: "**What's** this table **made of**?"
B: "It looks like glass, but it's actually made of plastic."

For *looks like*, see page 271

it's **worth** $199

its **real value is** $199

MORE EXAMPLES 🗩

"Gold is **worth** more than silver."

A: "This used Mercedes for sale on eBay is so cheap! It's only $12,000."
B: "How much is it **worth**?"
A: "It's **worth** $20,000!"

For *for sale*, see page 121

plug something **in**

connect something **to a power outlet**

MORE EXAMPLES

"I'll **plug in** the new TV so we can watch it."

"You can **plug** the iron **in** here. Please un-plug it when you're finished."

NOTE: unplug = remove the plug from the power outlet
NOTE: **plug** something **in**, **plug in** something, **plug** it **in**, NOT ~~plug in it~~

what if

what will happen if

Ask this when you are worried about something that might happen.

MORE EXAMPLES 🗩

A: "I don't have health insurance."
B: "**What if** you get sick?"

A: "Let's have the party outside."
B: "**What if** it rains?"
A: "If it rains, we can move inside."

ACROSS

2) "Will you hold my dog?" • "___ if he bites me?"
• "Don't worry. He's very friendly."
4) "I think we should take the train. You think we should fly. We don't see ___ ___ ___."
6) "You have a new car. Can I buy your old car?"
• "No. It's not ___ sale. I want to keep it."

DOWN

1) "What's your shirt ___ ___?" • "It's 100% cotton."
3) "Here's the radio. If you plug ___ ___, we can listen to it."
5) "I paid too much money for that watch! I paid $300, but it's ___ only $100."

For answers, see page 366

he **let** me go /
he **made** me run

he **allowed** me to go / he **forced** me to run

NOT ~~let me to go~~; NOT ~~made me to run~~

MORE EXAMPLES 💬

A: "My company **makes** us wear uniforms."
B: "Really? My company **lets** us wear jeans."

"My manager **let** me take two days off last week."

For *take two days off*, see page 65

look something **up**

find a piece of information **in**
a book or on the Internet

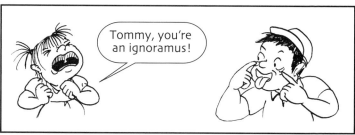

MORE EXAMPLES 🗩

A: "How did you get my phone number?"
B: "I **looked** it **up** in the phone book."

A: "I need the address of the hotel."
B: "I'll **look up** the address on the Internet."

NOTE: **look** something **up**, **look up** something, **look** it **up**, NOT ~~look up it~~

get rid of something

make something **go away**;
eliminate something

Get rid of that frog!

MORE EXAMPLES 🖝

A: "You bought a new car?"
B: "Yes, we **got rid of** our old car. We sold it."

"You can **get rid of** a toothache by putting ice on it."

must have done something

Say this when you guess about something that happened in the past, and you are quite sure.

MORE EXAMPLES 💬

"John isn't answering his phone. He **must have** gone out."

"Look! There's $20 on the floor. Someone **must have** dropped it."

shoot

This is a way to show anger or frustration.

MORE EXAMPLES 🗩

A: "Have you seen John?"
B: "He's gone for the day."
A: "Oh, **shoot**! I really needed to talk to him."

"**Shoot**! I just spilled coffee on my shirt."

For *gone for the day*, see page 55

Could you tell me where
something **is?**

NOT ~~Could you tell me where is something?~~

MORE EXAMPLES 🖝

A: "**Could you tell me where** the manager's office **is?**"

B: "It's on the second floor."

A: "**Could you tell me where** the nearest restaurant **is?**"

B: "There's a restaurant about two blocks from here."

For *two blocks from here*, see page 39

GRAB A PENCIL! · Puzzle #19

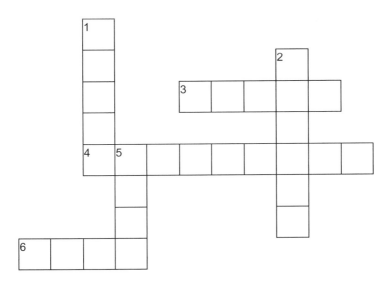

ACROSS
ACROSS
3) "We had ants in our kitchen. Then I used Jimco Ant Killer Powder, and we got ___ ___ the ants."
4) "Could you tell me where ___ ___ ___?" ▪ "Sure. The bank is on Main Street."
6) "When I was a child, my mother ___ me eat vegetables. She said, 'You must eat your vegetables!'"

DOWN
1) Rearrange these letters to find a way to express frustration or anger: othos
2) "If you don't understand a word, ___ it ___ in the dictionary."
5) "I put a tuna sandwich on the table. Now it's gone! My cat loves tuna. My cat must ___ eaten it."

For answers, see page 366

133

don't mention it

This is a polite response when someone thanks you.

MORE EXAMPLES 🗩

A: "Here's your umbrella. You forgot it."
B: "Oh, thank you!"
A: "**Don't mention it**."

A: "Thanks for mailing those letters for me."
B: "**Don't mention it**."

Would you mind do**ing** something?

Ask this to make a very polite request.

NOT ~~Would you mind to~~

Excuse me. Would you mind closing the window?

MORE EXAMPLES 🗨

"**Would you mind** mov**ing** your car out of the way? I want to park here."

A: "Sir, **would you mind** not smok**ing** here?"
B: "Sorry. I'll smoke outside."

For *move something out of the way*, see page 18

sold out

all sold so that **there is no more**

MORE EXAMPLES 🖝

"We couldn't go to the show because the tickets were **sold out**."

"The fish was **sold out**, so I bought chicken instead of fish."

For *instead of*, see page 173

half-way through

Say this when you have finished
50% of something.

MORE EXAMPLES 🖝

"This book is 1,000 pages long! I'm **half-way through**. I'm on page 500."

"He's **half-way through** his MBA program. It's a two-year program, and he just finished the first year."

how much longer

how much more time

MORE EXAMPLES 🗩

A: "She hasn't finished the job yet."
B: "**How much longer** will it take?"

A: "**How much longer** do you need to cook dinner? I'm hungry."
B: "Another 20 minutes. I'm only half-way through."

For *half-way through*, see page 137

take the highway
go on the highway

MORE EXAMPLES

"We got lost on our way here. We **took** the wrong street."

"Don't **take** Main Street during rush hour. You'll be stuck in traffic."

For *on our way,* see page 53
For *stuck in traffic,* see page 23

GRAB A PENCIL! · Puzzle #20

ACROSS
2) "How do I get to the airport?" ▪ "___ Bedford Street all the way."
3) "We have been waiting for Joe for 30 minutes! How ___ ___ should we wait?" ▪ "Let's wait five more minutes."
4) "I went to the store, but they didn't have any more milk. The milk was ___ ___."
5) "I don't want to go to the dentist alone. Would you ___ ___ with me?"

DOWN
1) "I have to photocopy 80 pages. I've already photocopied 40 pages, so I'm half-___ ___."
3) "Thanks for helping me." ▪ "Don't ___ it."

For answers, see page 366

double-check

check *again* when you are not sure about something

MORE EXAMPLES 🗩

"I think Ken's party is tomorrow night. But I'm not positive. I'll call him to **double-check**."

A: "Are you sure there are no mistakes in the report?"

B: "Yes, I checked and then I **double-checked**."

For *positive,* see page 159

a bad connection

an unclear phone connection

MORE EXAMPLES 🗨

"This is **a bad connection**. I can't hear you very well. Could you repeat that?"

"My battery is low, so we have **a bad connection**. We might get cut off."

For *get cut off,* see page 37

in that case

because of the thing you just said

Say this when you must change something
because you get new information.

MORE EXAMPLES 🗩

A: "Waiter, I'd like the steak please."
B: "I'm sorry. We've run out of steak."
A: "**In that case**, I'll have the spaghetti."

A: "Jack can't come to the meeting today."
B: "**In that case**, let's meet tomorrow."

For *run out of*, see page 186

Where is something held?

Ask this to learn the location of an event.

MORE EXAMPLES 🖛

A: "Last night we went to a piano concert."
B: "**Where was** it **held**?"
A: "At the Smith Theater."

A: "I take a painting class every Tuesday."
B: "**Where is** it **held**?"
A: "It's held at the College of Fine Arts."

it doesn't matter

it is not important

MORE EXAMPLES 🗨

A: "I forgot to mail your letter. Sorry."
B: "**It doesn't matter**. It wasn't urgent."

"**It doesn't matter** where we eat lunch as long as it's not expensive."

For *as long as,* see page 81

I **might**

It's possible that I **will**

NOT ~~Maybe I will~~

Are you going to wear a dress tonight?

I might. I might not. I might wear pants.

MORE EXAMPLES 🖝

A: "Why are you bringing your umbrella? It's not raining."
B: "It **might** rain later."

A: "Are you going to buy that car?"
B: "I **might**. I can't make up my mind."

For *make up my mind*, see page 45

ACROSS

4) "I looked in my bag, but I can't find my keys."
   ▪ "Why don't you ___-___? Look in your bag again."
5) "Are you going to the party?" ▪ "I ___ go. I'm not sure."
6) "We can't watch a movie. My DVD player is broken." ▪ "___ ___ case, let's watch TV."

DOWN

1) "Tom called me from the airport. I couldn't hear him clearly. We had a bad ___."
2) "I'm going to walk home." ▪ "But it's raining!" ▪ "It doesn't ___. I have an umbrella."
3) "Last night was our annual company dinner." ▪ "Where was it ___?" ▪ "At the Holton Hotel."

For answers, see page 366

Is this seat taken?

This is polite to ask before
sitting beside a stranger.

MORE EXAMPLES 🗩

A: "Excuse me. **Is this seat taken?**"
B: "No, go ahead."

A: "**Is this seat taken?**"
B: "Yes, sorry. I'm saving it for someone."

For *go ahead*, see page 110

play it by ear

do it *without* a plan

MORE EXAMPLES 💬

A: "What movie should we see?"
B: "Let's **play it by ear**. Let's go to the movie theater first, and *then* choose a movie."

"Don't book a hotel room. **Play it by ear**. Look for a hotel when you get to the city."

set up

establish; start

MORE EXAMPLES 🗨

"I work for a company, but next year I hope to **set up** my own business."

"I'm a computer programmer. I **set up** accounting programs for companies."

in those days / today

then / now

MORE EXAMPLES 💬

"I became a writer in the 1970's. **In those days** I used a typewriter, but **today** I use a computer."

"I went to Tate College. **In those days** I had no money. **Today** I own a beautiful home."

I didn't get your name

Say this when you didn't hear someone's name, or you can't remember it.

MORE EXAMPLES 🗨

"Who's that man in the blue jacket? **I didn't get** his **name**."

A: "This is Mr. Stevanoloulich."
B: "Mr. ...? Sorry, **I didn't get** your **name**."

nice to see you again

Say this when you see someone
who you don't see often.

NOT ~~Nice to meet you~~

MORE EXAMPLES 🗩

A: "Hi Ann. I haven't seen you for a long time."
B: "Yes, **nice to see you again**, Ahmed."

"Good-bye Jim. It was **nice to see you again**.
Please send my regards to your wife."

For *I haven't seen you for*, see page 187
For *send my regards*, see page 192

ACROSS

3) "We met last year." ▪ "Yes, I remember. It's nice to ___ you again."

4) "I got married 25 years ago. ___ ___ days, we lived with my parents, but now we have our own house."

5) "Who is that man? I just talked to him, but I didn't ___ his name."

DOWN

1) "What time should we serve dinner at the party?" ▪ "Whenever the guests get hungry. Let's play it ___ ___."

2) "I'd like to sit here. ___ this seat ___?" ▪ "No, it's not. You can sit here."

3) "Our office is in Boston. Next year we plan to ___ ___ another office in Chicago."

For answers, see page 366

it's on the tip of my tongue

I can *almost* remember it

MORE EXAMPLES 🗩

A: "What's the capital of Canada?"

B: "Otta... **It's on the tip of my tongue**. Otta... Ottawa!"

A: "Do you remember my address?"

B: "Sure, it's 22... wait, **it's on the tip of my tongue**... Elm Street?"

A: "Yes, that's right!"

give someone a ride

drive someone **to a place they need to go**

MORE EXAMPLES 🖝

A: "Could you **give** me **a ride** to school?"
B: "Sure, I'll drop you off on my way to work."

A: "How are you getting to the party?"
B: "Mary is **giving** me **a ride**."

For *drop you off*, see page 72
For *on my way*, see page 53
For *How are you getting to*, see page 344

have trouble with
something

Say this when something is a problem.

I'm having trouble with my car.

MORE EXAMPLES 🖝

"My son is **having trouble with** his chemistry homework. Can you help him?"

"I always **have trouble with** this key! It's difficult to unlock the door!"

For *it's difficult to,* see page 300

by far

by a large amount

Say this to show that something is
very different from other things.

MORE EXAMPLES 🖝

"This is the fastest printer we have **by far**.
All the others are much slower."

"Most camera shops charge 50 cents per
photo. But this shop charges only 20 cents!
That's the lowest price **by far**."

I'm positive

I'm 100% sure

MORE EXAMPLES 🗨

A: "I can't find the key."
B: "Are you sure you left it on the table?"
A: "**I'm positive**. I remember putting it there."

A: "Mr. Jackson still hasn't received my letter."
B: "Are you sure you sent it?"
A: "**I'm not positive**, but I think so."

For *left,* see page 232

I **can't figure out how to**

Say this when you can't understand
how to do something.

MORE EXAMPLES 🗩

A: "I **can't figure out how to** turn this radio on."
B: "Just press this button."

"Joe **can't figure out how to** use the fax machine. Could you give him a hand?"

For *give him a hand*, see page 176

ACROSS

5) "I'm ___ trouble ___ my printer. The paper keeps getting stuck."

6) "I'm going to walk to the bank." ▪ "My car is right here. I can give you a ___."

DOWN

1) "Pat is 34 years old. All of the other students are 19 or 20. Pat is the oldest ___ ___."

2) "Are you sure you locked the door?" ▪ "Yes, I'm ___."

3) "Why can't you print out the document?" ▪ "Because I can't figure ___ ___ to use the printer."

4) "Her name is Marina or Melina or... It's on the ___ ___ my tongue. Oh yes, it's Miranda!"

For answers, see page 366

something **works** / **doesn't work**

something **functions** / **doesn't function**

MORE EXAMPLES 🗩

"My camera **doesn't work**. I dropped it yesterday. I must have broken it."

A: "This radio is so old. Does it **work**?"
B: "Yes, it **works** well. Just plug it in."

For *must have,* see page 130
For *plug it in,* see page 124

suggest that he / you / we

NOT ~~suggest him to~~; NOT ~~suggest you to~~;
NOT ~~suggest us to~~

MORE EXAMPLES 🗨

A: "I need a lot of money."
B: "I **suggest that you** go to your bank.
   They can lend you money."

"His hair is too long, so I **suggested that he**
get a haircut."

NOTE: suggest that he put, get, go, etc.
NOT ~~suggest that he puts, gets, goes, etc.~~

For *lend*, see page 225

in May / on Tuesday, May 2 at 9 o'clock

in + month; on + day; at + time

MORE EXAMPLES 🗩

A: "When did she have the baby?"
B: "It was **in** July. In fact, it was **on** July 16 **at** 6 o'clock."

A: "Are you free next Wednesday?"
B: "No, but I'm free **on** Thursday."
A: "How about **at** 3 o'clock?"

NOTE: NOT ~~on next Wednesday~~

come off

become detached

Tom, look! The bumper is coming off!

MORE EXAMPLES 🗩

"I bought a cheap suitcase. The wheels **came off** after one week!"

"My house is in bad condition. The paint is **coming off** the walls. And last night, the door handle **came off** the door."

For *condition*, see page 92

a fortune

a lot of money

MORE EXAMPLES 🖛

"Last summer it rained every day. Umbrella companies made **a fortune**!"

"He spends **a fortune** on his son's education. It isn't worth it. His son never studies."

NOTE: made = earned

For *it isn't worth it*, see page 219

at the most

not more than

That's too expensive for me. I can spend $7,000 at the most.

MORE EXAMPLES 🔊

"The wedding hall is small, so we can invite 30 people **at the most** to our wedding."

"I can play tennis for one hour **at the most**. After an hour, I feel tired."

1		2			3	
				4		
		5				
6						

ACROSS

1) "I lost my wedding ring while I was swimming! I think it came ___ in the swimming pool."

5) "My brother wants to learn English." ▪ "I suggest ___ ___ watch American movies."

6) "My cell phone fell in the swimming pool and now it ___ work!"

DOWN

2) "I want to buy a piano, but I don't have enough money. Pianos cost a ___!"

3) "My wife buys expensive shoes, but I don't. I spend $30 ___ ___ most on shoes."

4) "My train leaves ___ Saturday ___ 7 o'clock. I bought the ticket ___ April."

For answers, see page 366

in the short term / in the long run

temporarily / over a long period of time

MORE EXAMPLES

"Covering the hole in your roof is okay **in the short term**. But **in the long run**, you will need a new roof."

"Smoking doesn't always hurt you when you're young. But **in the long run**, you develop health problems."

think it over

take time to think before deciding

MORE EXAMPLES 🗨

A: "Will you take that job?"
B: "I'm not sure. I need a few days to **think it over**."

"I've **thought it over** and I've made up my mind. I'm going to study engineering."

For *made up my mind*, see page 45

get something in writing

have a signed agreement or contract

MORE EXAMPLES 🗩

A: "He said he will pay me next month."
B: "You should **get** it **in writing**."

A: "You and I already have a verbal agreement."
B: "Yes, but I'd like to **get** our agreement **in writing**."

NOTE: verbal agreement = a spoken agreement

come with

be served with and included in the price of something

MORE EXAMPLES 🍃

"You don't need to order soup because your chicken **comes with** soup."

A: "Does the spaghetti **come with** a salad?"
B: "No, a salad costs extra."

instead of something

to replace something

MORE EXAMPLES

"We have a meeting on Friday, but I'll be very busy then. Could we meet on Thursday **instead of** Friday?"

"My fax machine is broken. Please email me **instead of** fax**ing** me."

NOTE: sometimes **instead of** + _**ing**

throw something away / put something away

put something in the trash / put something in a special storage place

MORE EXAMPLES 💬

"Those carrots are two months old. **Throw** them **away!**"

"My kids always **put away** their toys when they're finished playing."

NOTE: **throw** something **away**, **throw away** something, **throw** it **away**, NOT ~~throw away it~~
NOTE: **put** something **away**, **put away** something, **put** it **away**, NOT ~~put away it~~

GRAB A PENCIL! · Puzzle #25

ACROSS

5) "I'll invite Sally to the movies." ▪ "Sally is sick." ▪ "Then I'll invite Mary ___ ___ Sally."

6) "Right now I work at a restaurant. But in the long ___, I hope to open my own restaurant."

DOWN

1) "The pizzas are very good at this restaurant. They are only $6.99 and they ___ ___ soup and a salad."

2) "In business, never accept a spoken promise. Always ask for a contract. Get it ___ ___."

3) "These shoes are old and broken. Why don't you ___ them ___?"

4) "Do you want to buy this house?" ▪ "We'd like to think ___ ___ for a few days."

For answers, see page 366

give someone a hand

help someone

MORE EXAMPLES

A: "I can't reach the top shelf."
B: "Let me **give** you **a hand**."

"Fred had to photocopy 1,000 pages, so I **gave** him **a hand** with the job."

enough

adjective + enough / enough + noun

NOT ~~enough tall~~ /
NOT ~~space enough~~

MORE EXAMPLES

"I don't have **enough time** to call him to-day. I'm too busy."

A: "Can you print 100 pages an hour?"
B: "No, my printer isn't **fast enough**."

NOTE: noun = thing (book, man, house);
adjective = describing word (good, tall, old)

bring something up

start talking about something

MORE EXAMPLES 🔊

"Sam **brought up** the problem and then we all discussed it."

A: "Can we talk about the schedule?"
B: "Yes. I'm glad you **brought** it **up**."

NOTE: **bring** something **up**, **bring up** something, **bring** it **up**, NOT ~~bring up it~~

fine with me

I accept the suggestion

How about eating here?

Murray's Restaurant

It's fine with me.

Fine with me too.

MORE EXAMPLES 🗩

A: "Why don't we paint this wall green?"
B: "Okay. That's **fine with me**."

A: "Would it be possible to change the meeting to Thursday?"
B: "That's **fine with me,** but you'd better ask Frank too."

For *Would it be possible to*, see page 257

a table for three

Say this when you want the restaurant staff to find you a table.

MORE EXAMPLES 🗩

"We'd like **a table for** two in non-smoking, please."

"Could we have **a table for** four by the window, please?"

NOTE: non-smoking = the area where smoking is not allowed

ready to order

Say this when you want to order your meal.

MORE EXAMPLES 🍝

A: "Miss? We're **ready to order**."
B: "I'll be with you in one moment."

A: "Excuse me, I'm **ready to order**."
B: "Okay. What would you like?"

ACROSS

3) "I have a problem." ▪ "Please ___ ___ your problem at the meeting. We can discuss it then."

5) "I need help fixing my car. You know how to fix cars. Could you give me a ___?"

6) (at a restaurant) "Excuse me, Waiter. Can we have a table ___ four?"

DOWN

1) "This camera costs $99. I only have $70. I can't buy it. I don't have ___ money."

2) "Do you mind if I smoke?" ▪ "It's fine ___ ___, but ask the others too."

4) (at a restaurant) "Have you decided what you'd like?" ▪ "Yes, we are ___ ___ order."

For answers, see page 366

182

split the check

**each person pays the same amount
at a** restaurant

MORE EXAMPLES 🗩

A: "Who paid for dinner?"
B: "We each paid $20. We **split the check**."

A: "This dinner is on me."
B: "No, you paid last time. Let me pay."
A: "The bill is $150. I can't let you pay that much!"
B: "Okay, then let's **split the check**."

For *on me*, see page 22

the other day

a few days ago

MORE EXAMPLES 🗩

"I had a car accident **the other day** when I was driving to work."

A: "I saw Mr. White **the other day**."
B: "When?"
A: "I can't remember."

there is something left
something is remaining

MORE EXAMPLES 🗨

A: "**Is there** any pizza **left**?"
B: "Yes, **there are** two slices **left**."

"We ran out of paper yesterday. **There's** no
paper **left**."

For *ran out of*, see page 186

run out of something

use something **until it is finished**

We've run out of teabags.

MORE EXAMPLES 🗩

A: "Where are the stamps?"
B: "We **ran out of** them. I used the last one yesterday."

"We're **running out of** envelopes. We only have three left."

NOTE: **running out of** = *almost* finished

For *left*, see page 185

I haven't seen you for years

the last time I saw you **was** many years **ago**

MORE EXAMPLES

"I miss my family. **I haven't seen** them **for** six months."

"Is Tom in the office this week? **I haven't seen** him **for** a few days."

What are you up to these days?

tell me about your recent life

MORE EXAMPLES

A: "**What are you up to these days?**"
B: "I have my own company now."

A: "I haven't seen you for ages. **What are you up to these days?**"
B: "I'm still working for the same company."

NOTE: ages = a long time

For *I haven't seen you for,* see page 187

GRAB A PENCIL! · Puzzle #27

ACROSS
1) "How's Linda?" ▪ "I don't know. I never see her. I haven't ___ her ___ five years!"
4) "We need to buy eggs. There are only two ___ in the refrigerator."
5) "We need to buy sugar. We don't have any more. We ran ___ ___ sugar yesterday."

DOWN
1) "Our bill is $20, and there are four of us. If we ___ the check, we each pay $5."
2) "Anna called me the ___ day. I can't remember which day it was; maybe Tuesday or Wednesday."
3) "I haven't seen you for ages! What are you ___ ___ these days?" ▪ "I'm in college now."

For answers, see page 366

I'd better get going

Say this when you need to leave.

MORE EXAMPLES 🗨

"It's late. **I'd better get going**. But thank you for a very nice dinner."

A: "Would you like another coffee?"
B: "Actually, **I'd better get going** now."

keep in touch

continue to have contact

MORE EXAMPLES 🗩

"My brother lives in Italy. We **keep in touch** by phone."

A: "Do you **keep in touch** with your old classmates?"
B: "Yes, we email each other."

send my regards to someone

Say this if you want someone to give your greeting to another person.

MORE EXAMPLES 🗨

A: "How's your family?"
B: "Fine thanks."
A: "**Send my regards to** them."

A: "Andy **sends his regards to** you."
B: "Please **send my regards** back **to** him."

call someone back

phone someone **who tried phoning you earlier**

MORE EXAMPLES 💬

A: "Mr. Smith called you."
B: "I know. I tried to **call** him **back**, but he wasn't in the office."

"I don't have the information you need. I'll find it and **call** you right **back**."

NOTE: **call** someone **right back** = call someone back *very soon*

go through something

search or examine something **carefully**

MORE EXAMPLES 🗩

"I **went through** my bag, but I still can't find my keys!"

"I'm **going through** this report. I want to double-check for mistakes."

For *double-check*, see page 141

returning someone's **call**

Say this when you phone someone who tried phoning you earlier.

MORE EXAMPLES

A: "Hi Mary. I'm **returning** your **call**."
B: "Thanks Louis. I called you yesterday because..."

A: "May I speak to Don?"
B: "Can I ask what it's regarding?"
A: "Yes. I'm **returning** his **call**."

For *Can I ask what it's regarding*, see page 349

ACROSS

1) (on the phone) "You tried calling me last night, but I wasn't home. Now I'm ___ your call."
4) "Look at the time! I'd better ___ going. I have to meet my husband soon."
5) (on the phone) "I can't talk right now. I'll call you ___ later."

DOWN

1) "How is your sister?" • "She's fine." • "Please send my ___ to her."
2) "I want to go ___ all my clothes and throw away the clothes I never wear."
3) "Juan moved to Spain, but we still contact each other. We keep ___ ___ by email."

For answers, see page 367

on the other line

talking on a different phone line

MORE EXAMPLES 🗨

"When you called me, I was **on the other line**, so I couldn't talk to you."

A: "Can I speak to Ivan?"
B: "He's **on the other line**. Would you like to leave a message?"

on the right track

doing the right thing

MORE EXAMPLES 🗩

"We haven't succeeded yet, but we're **on the right track**."

A: "I want to get a better job, so I'm going to business school."
B: "You're **on the right track**."

almost all something

≈ **90% of** something

NOT ~~almost the cake~~

You ate almost all the cake! And almost all the cookies!

MORE EXAMPLES 🗩

"I'll be in the office **almost all** day. I'll just go out for lunch."

"Ernest Hemingway is my favorite writer. I've read **almost all** his books."

for the next four days

starting **now and continuing for** four days

MORE EXAMPLES 🗩

"We are fixing the elevator. **For the next** few hours, please use the stairs."

"Sam is on leave. **For the next** three weeks, Mary will be doing his job."

For *on leave*, see page 319

at three o'clock **sharp**

at exactly 3 o'clock; not 2:59 and not 3:01

MORE EXAMPLES 📣

"The meeting will start **at** 4 o'clock **sharp**, so please be on time."

"The boat leaves **at** 7:59 a.m. **sharp**. So if you arrive at 8 o'clock, you will be too late."

let someone know

give someone information

MORE EXAMPLES 🗩

A: "When are you going on vacation?"
B: "I'm not sure. I'll **let** you **know** soon."

"When you find out how much it costs, please **let** me **know**."

For *find out*, see page 258

GRAB A PENCIL! · Puzzle #29

ACROSS

2) "Every morning at 9:59, the store manager unlocks the door. The store opens at 10 o'clock ___."
3) "I had $100, but I spent $90. I spent almost ___ my money."
5) "Did you get the job?" ▪ "I'm not sure. The company will let ___ ___ next week."
6) "I want to be a singer. I take singing lessons every day." ▪ "You're on ___ ___ track."

DOWN

1) "Take this medicine every day. Start today and take it for five days." ▪ "Okay Doctor, I'll take it for ___ ___ five days."
4) (on the phone) "Ed can't talk to you now. He's on the other ___. He's talking to someone on another phone."

For answers, see page 367

203

How did something go?

Ask this to learn if something was successful.

MORE EXAMPLES

A: "**How did** your job interview **go**?"
B: "It went well. I think I'll get a job offer."

A: "**How did** your presentation **go**?"
B: "It went okay. I was a little nervous."

I'm **interested in** something

NOT ~~I interesting~~

MORE EXAMPLES 📢

A: "Why are you reading a book about Gandhi?"
B: "I'm **interested in** his life."

"My son is **interested in** learning karate."

NOTE: sometimes **interested in** + _ing

hang up

end a phone call by cutting the connection

Bye Mom.

Don't hang up! I need to talk to her.

MORE EXAMPLES 💬

A: "Is Mary still talking on the phone?"
B: "No, she just **hung up**."

"This is a bad connection. I'll **hang up** and call you back."

For *a bad connection*, see page 142
For *call you back*, see page 193

it's someone's turn

it's someone's **time** to do something

MORE EXAMPLES

"Monday is my day to feed the cat. Tuesday is your day. Today is Tuesday, so **it's** your **turn**."

"There's no toner left in the copier. I changed the toner last time. Now **it's** Dave's **turn**."

NOTE: toner = a dry ink powder used in printers and copiers

For *left*, see page 185

eight **feet long / wide / high**

NOT ~~long eight feet~~/ NOT ~~wide four feet~~/
NOT ~~high four feet~~

Dad, it's 8 feet long,
4 feet wide and
4 feet high! It's too big!

MORE EXAMPLES 💬

A: "How big is your office?"
B: "It's 20 **feet long** and 15 **feet wide**."

A: "How high is Mount Everest?"
B: "It's 29,035 **feet high**!"

move on

begin a new topic

We often use this in meetings.

MORE EXAMPLES 🗩

"We can't solve this problem right now, so let's **move on** to the next problem."

"We've been talking about this for an hour! We should **move on**."

ACROSS

3) "Why don't you like your history class?" ▪ "I'm not interested ___ history."
4) "Sam cooked on Wednesday. Marcy cooked on Thursday. It was my ___ on Friday."
5) "We have answered the first question. Let's ___ ___ to the second question."
6) "After I finish this phone call, I will ___ ___ the phone and start working."

DOWN

1) "Look! That snake is longer than a car!" ▪ "Yes, actually it's 16 ___ ___!"
2) "How ___ your job interview ___?" ▪ "It went well. We talked for a long time."

For answers, see page 367

wrap up

finish a meeting

MORE EXAMPLES 🖝

A: "Sorry I missed the meeting. What time did you **wrap up**?"
B: "At 5 o'clock."

"I'd like to **wrap up** this meeting by 6 o'clock, so let's move on to the next point now."

For *by 6 o'clock,* see page 117
For *move on,* see page 209

211

there's no point

there's no reason

Say this when it is not useful to do something.

MORE EXAMPLES 🗩

A: "Let's go to the mall."
B: "**There's no point**. It's closed now."

A: "Should I fix this printer?"
B: "No, it's too old. **There's no point in** fix-**ing** it. It will just break again."

NOTE: sometimes **there's no point in + _ing**

calm down

become relaxed

MORE EXAMPLES 🗩

A: "I'm so angry at Maria. I'm going to talk to her right now!"

B: "You should **calm down** before you talk to her."

"I always feel nervous before a job interview. So I sit quietly and try to **calm down** first."

Can I make a suggestion?

You can ask this before suggesting something.

MORE EXAMPLES 🔊

A: "I don't like taking the bus."
B: **"Can I make a suggestion?"**
A: "Okay."
B: "Why don't you take the train instead of the bus?"

A: "This office is dark."
B: **"Can I make a suggestion?"**
A: "Sure."
B: "Let's paint it yellow."

For *instead of*, see page 173

do something **in** five days
it takes five days **to complete** something

MORE EXAMPLES 🗩

"She can run five miles **in** 30 minutes!"

"He ate six burgers **in** five minutes! No wonder he's sick!"

For *no wonder*, see page 20
For a different meaning of *in*, see page 12

for the time being

at this time only; not forever

MORE EXAMPLES 🗩

"We plan to buy a house, but **for the time being** we're living with my parents."

"I'm working as a waiter **for the time being**. But I hope to become a doctor."

	1		2			3

(crossword grid)

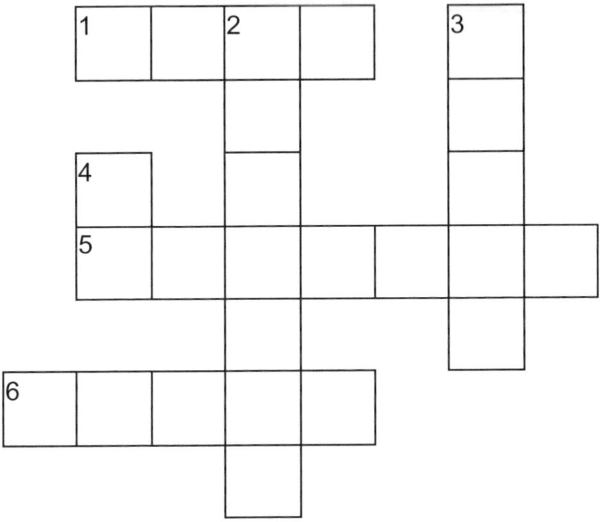

ACROSS
1) "Kids, stop running around the house! Please calm ___ and sit quietly."
5) "You should paint your house." ▪ "There's ___ ___ in painting it. I'm moving next month."
6) "I don't like my hairstyle!" ▪ "Can I ___ ___ suggestion?" ▪ "Sure." ▪ "Get it cut short."

DOWN
2) "The meeting was so long. We finally ___ up at 8 p.m.!"
3) "My car is at the repair shop, so I'm using a bicycle for the time ___."
4) "How long does it take to walk to the bank?" ▪ "I can walk there ___ five minutes."

For answers, see page 367

I see your point

I understand your opinion or feelings

I can't work with these things all around me!

Yes, I see your point but it's just for a few days.

MORE EXAMPLES 🗨

A: "If you buy a car, you won't have enough money to buy a house."

B: "**I see your point**, but I need a car to get to work."

A: "You often borrow my car and use all the gas! Gas is expensive."

B: "Yes, **I see your point**. I'll buy gas next time."

it's not worth it

it requires too much effort for a small result

MORE EXAMPLES 💬

A: "Are you going to paint your house?"
B: "No. **It's not worth it**. We are moving next year."

A: "If you clean my house, I'll give you five bucks."
B: "Five bucks? No thanks. **It's not worth it**."

NOTE: bucks = dollars

can afford / can't afford

have enough money / don't have enough money

MORE EXAMPLES 🖝

"I **can't afford** a car, so I bought a bicycle."

"Big companies **can afford** to buy any computer system that they want."

the same as

NOT ~~same like~~

MORE EXAMPLES 🗩

A: "I'm going to order a burger."
B: "I'll have **the same as** you."

A: "Is your new office bigger than your old one?"
B: "No. It's **the same** size **as** the old office."

any minute now

very soon

It's going to rain any minute now.

MORE EXAMPLES 🗩

"Fred is outside parking his car. He'll be here **any minute now**."

"Would everyone please sit down? Ivan is going to start the meeting **any minute now**."

pull strings

use personal contacts to get something

MORE EXAMPLES

A: "How did he become vice president of the company?"

B: "His father is the president. His father **pulled** some **strings**."

A: "I'd like to work for ABC Company."

B: "My uncle works there."

A: "Maybe he can **pull** a few **strings** for me."

ACROSS
1) "Let's not leave at 8 o'clock. There will be less traffic at 10." ▪ "I see your _____. Let's leave at 10."
4) "Those shoes cost $99. I only have $50. I can't ___ those shoes."
5) "My friend works at this restaurant. Maybe he can pull some ___ and get us a good table."

DOWN
2) "My car is a Firebird." ▪ "I have ___ same car ___ you! My car is a Firebird too!"
3) "The movie theater is 20 miles from here." ▪ "Drive 20 miles just to see a movie? It's not ___ it."
4) "Please wait near the door. The taxi will be here ___ minute now."

For answers, see page 367

lend someone something

give something to someone **for a short time** — they will return it later

NOT ~~Could you borrow me~~

MORE EXAMPLES 🖋

"I **lent** Susan my jacket, but she never gave it back to me. She borrowed it from me last year!"

A: "I forgot to bring my cell phone."
B: "Here, I can **lend** you my phone."

within the hour

during the next hour

How long will it take to fix?

Maybe 10 minutes. Maybe 30 minutes. Maybe 50 minutes. It will be ready within the hour.

MORE EXAMPLES 🗩

"If you take the medicine now, you'll start to feel better **within the hour**."

"I'm going to the bank now. I'll be back **within the hour**."

For *back*, see page 264

go over something

check the details of something

MORE EXAMPLES 🖝

"Let's **go over** the travel arrangements. Your flight departs on Tuesday at 9:35 p.m. and ..."

"Make sure you **go over** the contract carefully before you sign it."

For *make sure,* see page 353

How's something coming along?

tell me about the progress of something that is *not* finished

MORE EXAMPLES

A: "**How's** your project **coming along**?"
B: "It's coming along fine."

A: "**How's** the report **coming along**?"
B: "We are half-way through."

For *half-way through*, see page 137

What's something for?

What is the purpose of something?

MORE EXAMPLES 🗩

A: "**What are** these machines **for**?"
B: "For making bread."

A: "**What's** this key **for**?"
B: "It's for the bathroom."

watch out

be careful of something that can be dangerous

Watch out for that saw!

MORE EXAMPLES 🖝

"**Watch out**! There's a hole in the road!"

"When you swim in the ocean, **watch out** for sharks."

ACROSS

2) "If you ride your bicycle on that street, please watch ___ for cars."

4) "It's 3 o'clock. I'm leaving sometime before 4 o'clock. I'm leaving ___ the hour."

6) "The numbers in our sales report look too low. Let's ___ ___ the numbers again."

DOWN

1) "How's your homework ___ along?" ▪ "Okay, Dad. I'm almost finished."

3) "I don't have a pen." ▪ "Here, I'll ___ ___ mine."

5) "What's this machine ___?" ▪ "It's for cleaning my car."

For answers, see page 367

leave something somewhere

let something **stay** somewhere;
forget something somewhere

MORE EXAMPLES 🗩

"I think I **left** my glasses on your desk."

A: "Where should I put this book?"
B: "Just **leave** it on the table. I'll put it away later."

For *put it away*, see page 174

call in sick

phone your boss to say you can't come to work because you're sick

MORE EXAMPLES 🗩

A: "Where's Bob? He's not at his desk."
B: "He **called in sick**."

"Susie **called in sick** today, so the sales department is short by one person."

For *short by*, see page 267

Can I have a word with you?

Can I speak to you for a short time?

MORE EXAMPLES

A: "**Can I have a word with you?**"
B: "Yes."
A: "We have to change the time of the meeting."

A: "**Can I have a word with you?**"
B: "Can you wait five minutes? I'm on the phone."

in a row

one thing directly after another thing

MORE EXAMPLES 🖜

"We went to Japan three years **in a row**. In 2004, 2005 and 2006."

"I exercised on Monday, Tuesday, Wednesday and Thursday. Is it healthy to exercise four days **in a row**?"

pick someone **up**

stop to get someone

MORE EXAMPLES 🗩

A: "How did you get to the doctor?"
B: "My husband **picked** me **up** at work and drove me."

"Rob's plane arrives at 4:30 p.m. tomorrow. I'll **pick** him **up** at the airport."

in luck / out of luck

lucky / unlucky

MORE EXAMPLES 🗪

A: "Would it be possible to see the doctor today?"

B: "You're **in luck.** A patient just canceled. You can come in at 2 o'clock."

"Oh no! We're **out of luck**. The store has already closed."

For *Would it be possible,* see page 257

ACROSS

1) "I need to speak to you for a few minutes. Can I have a ___ ___ you?"
5) "David gave me flowers on Friday, Saturday and Sunday." ▪ "Wow! Three days in ___ ___."
6) "I have a car so I will ___ you ___ at your house and drive you to the party."

DOWN

2) "I'd like to buy your car." ▪ "Sorry, you're ___ ___ luck. I just sold it."
3) "Joe can't come to work today because his tooth hurts. He called ___ ___."
4) "When you finish eating, don't ___ your dishes on the table. Please wash them."

For answers, see page 367

last three hours

continue for three hours

That movie was so long! It lasted 3 hours!

CINEMA ROOM 2

THE END

MORE EXAMPLES 🗩

A: "How long did the Second World War **last**?"
B: "It **lasted** six years, from 1939 to 1945."

A: "I hope the meeting doesn't **last** long."
B: "I think it will **last** about an hour."

For a different meaning of *last*, see page 244

get something done

finish something

MORE EXAMPLES 🗩

A: "When can you **get** the job **done**?"
B: "I can **get** it **done** by Friday."

"I can't **get** everything **done** today. I'll finish
  tomorrow."

For *by Friday*, see page 117

take longer than
someone **expected**
need more time than originally planned

MORE EXAMPLES 🗩

"I thought it would take two hours to drive to your house, but it took three hours. It **took longer than** I **expected**."

"I was supposed to finish this job today, but it's **taking longer than** I **expected**. I'll finish it tomorrow."

For *supposed to*, see page 305

have a sense of humor

enjoy funny things; enjoy laughing

MORE EXAMPLES 🗩

"I'd like to marry a man who **has a sense of humor**."

"It's important to **have a sense of humor** when life gets stressful."

can't get something
down / in / out / open

Say this when something is difficult to do.

MORE EXAMPLES

"My disc is stuck in my computer! I **can't get** it **out**!"

"My suitcase is full. I **can't get** my shoes **in**."

last 20 years

can function or **can be used for** 20 years

I used good wood. These cabinets will last 20 years.

MORE EXAMPLES 🗩

"I buy leather shoes because leather **lasts** a long time."

"I bought a cheap radio. It **lasted** six months. Then it broke."

For a different meaning of *last,* see page 239

ACROSS

1) "Paul's parties are always fun. They usually ___ all night long."
4) "I'm surprised it took you two months to write that report!" ▪ "Yes, it took longer than I ___."
5) "Lillian never laughs or makes jokes. She has no sense of ___."

DOWN

1) "If you keep your medicine in the refrigerator, it will ___ a long time."
2) "I haven't finished building your table." ▪ "Can you ___ it done by tomorrow?"
3) "There is some paper stuck in my printer. I can't ___ it ___."

For answers, see page 367

I'm sorry to hear...

When something bad happens to someone, say this to show you care.

MORE EXAMPLES 🗩

A: "**I'm sorry to hear** about your car accident."

B: "Thanks. I'm feeling better now."

A: "My dog died."

B: "**I'm sorry to hear** that. I know how much you loved your dog."

Would you prefer a or b?

Do you want a or b?

Ask this when you give someone a choice.

MORE EXAMPLES 💬

A: "**Would you prefer** coffee **or** tea?"
B: "Coffee, please."

A: "**Would you prefer** to meet at my office **or** yours?"
B: "It's up to you."

For *it's up to you*, see page 338

from now on

starting now and continuing forever

MORE EXAMPLES 🗩

"I just won $10,000! **From now on**, I'm going to take taxis, not buses!"

"Judy is our new receptionist. **From now on**, she will answer the phone."

that's funny

that's strange

MORE EXAMPLES 🗩

A: "Did you get my letter?"
B: "No."
A: "**That's funny**. I mailed it two weeks ago."

A: "Sandra isn't here yet."
B: "**That's funny**. She called me two hours ago and said she was on her way."

For *ago,* see page 46
For *on her way,* see page 53

there's nothing I can do (about it)

Say this when you cannot help someone.

MORE EXAMPLES 🖝

A: "I want to take the 2 o'clock train!"

B: "But, I told you it's fully booked. **There's nothing I can do**."

A: "Taxi Driver, please drive faster!"

B: "**There's nothing I can do**! We're stuck in traffic."

For *stuck in traffic*, see page 23

I'd better let you go

Say this to end a phone call politely.

Mrs. Kobori, I'd better let you go now.

Okay. Bye Sue. See you soon.

TALK TALK TALK TALK

MORE EXAMPLES 🖅

A: "**I'd better let you go** now."
B: "Okay. Keep in touch."
A: "I will. Bye."

A: "I'm sure you're busy. **I'd better let you go.**"
B: "Okay. Nice talking to you."

For *keep in touch*, see page 191

251

ACROSS
1) "It didn't rain, but the street is wet. That's ___." ▪ "You're right, that is strange!"
5) "I'm sorry ___ ___ your mother is sick. I hope she gets better soon."
6) "Please lower the price!" ▪ "I'm sorry. There's nothing I can ___ ___ ___. You have to speak to the boss."

DOWN
2) "I just smoked my last cigarette! I quit! From ___ ___, I will not smoke."
3) "How will we get downtown? Would you ___ ___ take the train or the bus?"
4) (on the phone) "Jane, I know you're busy. I'd better ___ you ___ now."

For answers, see page 367

look into something

investigate; research

I'm going to Shanghai next week.

SHANGHAI LIGHTING FAIR
DATE: 10.7
ADD: EX...

I'll look into hotels for you.

SEARCH: HOTELS IN SHANGHAI GO

MORE EXAMPLES 💬

"We just moved to a new city. We're **looking into** schools for our children."

A: "There's a problem with my bill."
B: "I'll **look into** the problem right away."

For *right away*, see page 31

reach someone

contact someone **by phone, email, fax, etc**.

You can reach me on my mobile, or at the Shanghai Hotel at 0086-21-338-3245, or by fax at 0086-21-868-4572, or by email or...

MORE EXAMPLES 🖝

A: "How can I **reach** you?"
B: "You can email me at this address."

"I'll be away on business for a few days, so you won't be able to **reach** me at the office."

For *away on business*, see page 262

get by

manage but with difficulty

MORE EXAMPLES 🗩

"My car broke down. I have to **get by** with my bicycle for a few days."

"We don't have much money, but we can **get by** if we don't spend much."

How long does it take to get to a place?

How much time is needed to arrive at a place?

MORE EXAMPLES 🗩

A: "**How long does it take to get to** Montreal from Toronto?"
B: "It takes about five hours."

A: "**How long does it take to get to** the bank?"
B: "Not long. It's a five-minute walk."

Would it be possible for someone to...?

This is a polite request.

Say this when you don't know if someone can help you.

MORE EXAMPLES 🗩

"**Would it be possible for** me **to** see the doctor today? I don't have an appointment."

A: "**Would it be possible for** you **to** lend me $300?"
B: "$300! That's a lot of money!"

For *lend*, see page 225

257

find out

get a piece of information

MORE EXAMPLES 🗩

A: "Let's go see that new movie tonight."
B: "Okay. I'll **find out** when it starts."

A: "How old is Jane?"
B: "I don't know, but I can **find out**. I'll ask her sister."

ACROSS

3) "If you need to speak to me, you can ___ me at home on most evenings."

4) "Teacher, a student is crying!" ▪ "Thank you. I'll look ___ the problem right now."

5) "I can't speak English well, but I can ___ by."

6) "I'm going to Boston next week. ___ ___ be possible for me stay at your house?"

DOWN

1) "How long does it ___ to ___ to the airport?" ▪ "About 30 minutes by car."

2) "When does his flight arrive?" ▪ "I don't know, but I'll ___ ___. I'll call the airline."

For answers, see page 367

How long have you been in this place?

Ask this to know the amount of time spent in the place someone is *now*.

MORE EXAMPLES 💬

A: "**How long have you been in** Hong Kong?"
B: "I've been here for six months, but I still can't find a job!"

A: "**How long have you been in** this country?"
B: "For five years. I grew up in Sri Lanka and moved here five years ago."

For *ago*, see page 46

What does this mean?

NOT ~~What mean this?~~; NOT ~~This mean what?~~

MORE EXAMPLES 🖝

A: "**What does** 'large' **mean**?"
B: "It means 'big'."

A: "**What does** 'insatiable' **mean**?"
B: "I don't know. Look it up in the dictionary."

For *look it up*, see page 128

away on business

in another city or country on a business trip

Hi Mary. I haven't seen Alan this week.

He's away on business in China.

MORE EXAMPLES 🗨

A: "Are you free next week?"
B: "No, I'll be **away on business**."

A: "I tried calling you last week, but I couldn't reach you."
B: "I was **away on business**."

For *reach*, see page 254

should have done something

Say this when something was a good idea, but you didn't do it. You made a mistake and now it's too late.

MORE EXAMPLES ✏

"Fred wanted to marry you, but you said no. Now he's very successful. You **should have** married him!"

"The copier is broken because you put in too much paper. You **shouldn't have** put in so much paper."

For *successful*, see page 309

someone **is back**

someone **has returned from somewhere**

Mr. Lee is back.

MORE EXAMPLES 🐾

A: "Miss French went to the bank. **Is** she **back**?"

B: "No, she **isn't back** yet."

"My father was in the hospital for a few days, but now he**'s back** home."

by the way

Say this to introduce a different topic.

MORE EXAMPLES 💬

A: "Are you ready to go to lunch?"
B: "Yes, let's go. **By the way**, your mother called."

"...then we visited Paris and then we went to London. **By the way**, how's your sister?"

ACROSS

1) "How long ___ you ___ in this city?" ▪ "I've been here for seven months."
3) "We have a test today, but I didn't study! I should ___ studied last night."
5) "What ___ 'speedy' ___?" ▪ "'Speedy' means 'fast'."
6) "Your sister went to Mexico. Is she still there?" ▪ "No, she's ___."

DOWN

2) "My husband often travels for his job. In fact, he's ___ ___ business right now. He's in Brazil."
4) "Let's print these documents now. By ___ ___, I'm having a party next Friday."

For answers, see page 367

266

short by

Say this when you don't have enough.
This shows how much you need.

MORE EXAMPLES 🗩

"We need 10 players for our football game. We have eight players, so we're **short by** two."

A: "My cash register is **short by** $15."
B: "You must have given a customer too much change."

For *must have*, see page 130

Have you been waiting long?

This is a polite question to ask someone waiting for you.

MORE EXAMPLES 🗩

A: "**Have you been waiting long?**"
B: "No, just a few minutes."

"I'm sorry to keep you waiting. **Have you been waiting long?**"

Will that be all?

Is that the only thing you want?

Servers ask this in restaurants.

MORE EXAMPLES 🗩

A: "I'll have a salad and an iced tea, please."
B: "**Will that be all?**"
A: "Yes, that's it, thank you."

A: "I'd like a cheeseburger to go, please."
B: "**Will that be all?**"
A: "No. And a Diet Coke, too."

For *that's it*, see page 59
For *to go*, see page 270

For here or to go?

Do you want to eat/drink here in the restaurant, or do you want to take it away?

Servers ask this in restaurants.

MORE EXAMPLES 🗩

A: "One cheeseburger, please."
B: "Is that **for here or to go?**"
A: "It's to go."

A: "I'd like two coffees, please."
B: "**For here or to go?**"
A: "For here, please."

look / look like

look + adjective / look like + noun

MORE EXAMPLES 💬

A: "You **look** tired."
B: "That's because I worked late every night this week."

A: "My new haircut is too short. I **look like** a boy."
B: "No, you **look** beautiful."

NOTE: noun = thing (book, man, house);
adjective = describing word (good, tall, old)

at least 21

21 **or more than** 21

MORE EXAMPLES 💬

A: "I wonder how much that jacket costs."
B: "**At least** $200. Maybe even $300! It's made of leather."

"That piano is heavy! You need **at least** four people to help you carry it."

For *made of*, see page 122

GRAB A PENCIL! · Puzzle #39

ACROSS

1) "To buy a house, you need $100,000 or more.
   You need ___ ___ $100,000."
3) "Thanks for waiting for me. Have you ___ waiting ___?" ▪ "No, only about five minutes."
5) "One coffee, please." ▪ "For here or ___ ___?"
   ▪ "I'll drink it here."

DOWN

2) "I need a 10-foot ladder. This one is eight feet
   long. This ladder is ___ ___ two feet."
3) "I'd like two hotdogs, please." ▪ "Will that ___
   ___?" ▪ "No, I'd like an iced tea too."
4) "My grandmother is old, but she ___ young
   because her skin is so soft."

For answers, see page 367

get back to someone

contact someone *as a reply* by phone, email, fax, etc.

MORE EXAMPLES 🗩

"I don't have that information right now. I'll **get back to** you later."

"Please **get back to** me by email or phone."

as far as I know

based on the information I have

Say this when you might be wrong.

MORE EXAMPLES 🗩

A: "Is Ali going to the meeting?"
B: "Yes. **As far as I know**, he's going. Bob told me everyone is going."

"There was a fire at the bank! **As far as I know**, nobody was hurt. That's what I heard on the radio."

How was something?

It's polite to ask about someone's recent experience.

Say this to know if it was good or bad.

MORE EXAMPLES 💬

A: "**How was** your vacation?"
B: "It was great, thanks."

A: "**How was** the conference?"
B: "Interesting. There were a lot of good speakers."

show someone around

take someone for a tour

Let me show you around.

This is our new product line.

...and this is our shipping department.

MORE EXAMPLES 🗩

"Welcome to Boston. I'll **show** you **around** the city tonight."

"We're interested in buying this house. Could you **show** us **around**?"

For *interested in*, see page 205

stand for

mean

Say this when only the first letters
of words are used.

MORE EXAMPLES

"U.S.A. **stands for** United States of America."

A: "What does FYI **stand for**?"
B: "It **stands for** 'for your information'."

make yourself / yourselves at home

please feel relaxed and comfortable

Say this to welcome guests to your home.

MORE EXAMPLES 🗩

"Hi James. Come in and **make yourself at home**. Let me take your coat."

A: "May I use your phone?"
B: "Go ahead. **Make yourself at home**."

For *go ahead*, see page 110

ACROSS
4) "I need Gloria's phone number." ▪ "Okay. I'll find it. Then I'll get ___ ___ you."
5) "We have a visitor from Canada. Last night I ___ him ___ our city."
6) "Is there a meeting today?" ▪ "Yes, as ___ ___ I know it's at 3 o'clock. That's what Bob told me."

DOWN
1) "Welcome to our house, Steve. Please relax and make ___ ___ home."
2) "___ ___ the party last night?" ▪ "It was fun."
3) "C.O.D. ___ ___ 'cash on delivery'."

For answers, see page 367

help yourself / yourselves

serve your own food or drink

Please help yourselves.

MORE EXAMPLES 🐷

A: "Can I have some more soup?"
B: "Sure. Could you **help yourself**? I have to cut the cake."

"Ladies, if you'd like tea or coffee, please **help yourselves**."

back and forth

in one direction, then in the opposite direction — repeated many times

MORE EXAMPLES 🗨

"That was a long tennis game. The ball went **back and forth** for two hours!"

"We emailed **back and forth** for six months before we met."

short notice

without much advance warning

MORE EXAMPLES 💬

"Could you type this letter for me? I know it's **short notice**, but I need it in 20 minutes."

A: "Can you repair my car today?"
B: "No, sorry, I can't do it on **short notice**. I have to repair a lot of cars today."

NOTE: do something *on* **short notice**

come up with something

produce an idea or solution

MORE EXAMPLES 🗨

"Those birds keep eating my flower seeds. I need to **come up with** a solution to the problem."

"Carl **came up with** a great idea for our presentation!"

hands-on experience

experience where you learn by doing something, not by studying

MORE EXAMPLES 🖙

"I study cooking, but I work as a waiter. This gives me **hands-on experience** in the restaurant business."

"I'm an architect now, but first I worked as a builder. That **hands-on experience** taught me a lot."

once every four years

NOT ~~four years once~~

MORE EXAMPLES 🗨

A: "I go jogging once a week."
B: "I only go **once every** two week**s**."

"The earth goes all the way around the sun **once every** 365 day**s**."

For *once a week*, see page 363

ACROSS

3) "I never took a computer class. I learned how to use computers through ___-___ experience."

4) "If you'd like a piece of cake, go into the kitchen and ___ ___."

6) "There were mice in our house. Then we came ___ ___ a solution. We got a cat!"

DOWN

1) "Can you write that report today?" ▪ "No, I can't do it on short ___. I need more time."

2) "We have a store downtown and a store in the suburbs. I manage both stores, so I drive ___ and ___ a lot."

5) "How often do you see your parents?" ▪ "I see them once ___ three weeks."

For answers, see page 367

Could you press 15?

Ask this in an elevator if you
can't reach the buttons.

MORE EXAMPLES 💬

A: "Which floor would you like?"
B: "**Could you press** seven, please?"

"**Could you press** six, please? I can't reach
it. Thanks."

Can I get by?

Ask this when you need someone
to move so you can go past them.

MORE EXAMPLES 🗩

A: "**Can I get by**, please? I have to catch a
train."
B: "Oh, sorry."

"Excuse me. **Can I get by?** I need to get off
the bus here."

For *get off*, see page 303

I'd recommend something

Say this to suggest something.

NOT ~~I recommend you to buy the Imax~~

MORE EXAMPLES 🗩

A: "Do you know any good French restaurants?"

B: "Yes, **I'd recommend** Chez Pierre."

A: "I need exercise. What should I do?"

B: "**I'd recommend** swimm**ing**."

NOTE: sometimes **recommend** +_**ing**

I don't know offhand

I don't have the information in my memory

Say this when you need to go
and find the answer.

MORE EXAMPLES 🗩

A: "How many people live in London?"
B: "**I don't know offhand**. I'll look it up on the Internet."

A: "Do you know Sam's phone number?"
B: "**I don't know** it **offhand**. It's in my address book."

For *look it up*, see page 128

have something done

Say this when *you* arrange something,
but *someone else* does it.

I need them tomorrow.

Tom, can you deliver 150 Imax lights tomorrow?

I'll have your lights delivered tomorrow.

MORE EXAMPLES 🗩

"There were workers in my house yesterday. I **had** the walls painted and I **had** the air conditioner repaired."

"We make radios, but we don't make the small parts. We **have** the parts made by another company."

move something **up**

change a plan **to an earlier time**

MORE EXAMPLES 🗩

"The deadline was Friday, but they **moved** it **up** to Thursday."

A: "Lunch is scheduled for 2 o'clock."
B: "That's a bit late. Can we **move** it **up** to one o'clock?"

NOTE: a bit = a little

ACROSS

1) "Which pasta dish is the best?" ▪ "I'd ___ the spaghetti with meatballs."
5) (on an elevator) "Could you ___ five, please?"
6) "Did you repair your car yourself?" ▪ "No, I ___ my car repaired at Tony's Auto Repair."

DOWN

2) "How old is Tina?" ▪ "I don't know ___. I'll look in her file and find out."
3) "The meeting is scheduled for next Friday, but let's ___ it ___ to this Wednesday."
4) "Excuse me, you are standing in front of me and I need to go past you. Can I ___ ___?"

For answers, see page 368

the week after next

the week after next week

NOT ~~next next week~~

MORE EXAMPLES 🖝

"My exam is **the week after next**, so I have to study hard next week."

"We can't get it done by next week, but we can get it done by **the week after next**."

For *get it done*, see page 240
For *by,* see page 117

I wish you all the best

Say this to wish someone happiness and success in their future or with a big project.

I wish you all the best, Margaret.

MORE EXAMPLES 💬

"Good-bye students. **I wish you all the best** next year."

"**I wish you all the best** with your new business. I'm sure it will be a success!"

if I were you, I'd...

Say this to give advice by imagining you are in the other person's situation.

MORE EXAMPLES 💬

A: "My salary is low and I don't enjoy my job."

B: "**If were you, I'd** look for another job."

A: "We've repaired our fax machine twice this year."

B: "**If I were you, I'd** buy a new one."

in other words

Say this if you need to repeat
something a different way.

MORE EXAMPLES 🗩

"A five-year-old child could understand this computer program. **In other words**, it's very easy."

"Employees are expected to have completed all duties prior to departure. **In other words**, finish your work before you go home."

tell someone

NOT ~~tell to someone~~; NOT ~~tell that~~

The doctor told me to exercise. I told him that I hate exercise.

MORE EXAMPLES 🗩

"She **told him** to wait. He **told her** that he couldn't wait."

"I **told the kids** to clean up their rooms. Please **tell them** again!"

it's easy to /
it's difficult to

NOT ~~I'm easy to~~ / NOT ~~I'm difficult to~~

It's easy to eat.
It's difficult to exercise.

MORE EXAMPLES 🖝

"**It's easy to** get to the airport. Just follow the signs."

"**It's difficult** for me **to** read without my glasses."

GRAB A PENCIL! · Puzzle #43

ACROSS
3) "I go to bed very late, so it's ___ ___ wake up early."
5) "Good luck, John! I wish you all ___ ___ in your new job."
6) "I'm on vacation for three weeks: this week, next week, and the week ___ ___."

DOWN
1) "I ___ Michael that you want to see him."
2) "Your son has high emotional intelligence. In other ___, he's kind and caring."
4) "Your car is 20 years old. If ___ ___ you, I'd buy a new car."

For answers, see page 368

give up

quit; stop doing something

MORE EXAMPLES

"I called him three times, but he never answered the phone. In the end, I **gave up**."

"I feel healthier now because I **gave up** smok**ing** last year."

NOTE: sometimes **give up** + **_ing**

get on / get off / get in / get out

get on / get off = for buses, trains and planes
get in / get out = for cars and taxis

Could you tell me how to get to the circus?

TRAIN TICKETS

Get off the train at Westwood Station. Then get on the 160 bus and get off at High Street. Then take a taxi and get out at Ash Street.

MORE EXAMPLES 🗩

"I was wearing my glasses when I **got on** the plane. I lost them when I **got off** the plane or when I **got in** the taxi!"

"Taxi Driver, I'd like to **get out** at the next street, please."

even though

Say this when you show two
contrasting or opposite ideas.

MORE EXAMPLES 💬

"**Even though** he's rich and successful,
he's not a happy person."

"ABC Printing Company is very good. So
even though they charge a lot, we use the
company."

was / were supposed to

Say this to talk about a plan that *didn't* happen.

MORE EXAMPLES

"I **was supposed to** go to the meeting. I planned to go, but I didn't. I was tied up."

"We **were supposed to** finish this last month, but it's still not complete."

For *tied up*, see page 15

take a chance

do something that might result in danger or failure

MORE EXAMPLES 🗩

"The mountain was icy and dangerous, but we **took a chance** and climbed up."

"We spent $10,000 on advertising. We **took a chance**, but it didn't work. It didn't increase sales."

on second thought

Say this when you change your decision.

MORE EXAMPLES 🖝

"Let's meet at the library. **On second thought**, let's meet at the coffee shop because the library is closed."

A: "I'm going to buy this tie."
B: "It's $300."
A: "$300? **On second thought**, I think I'll buy a different one."

GRAB A PENCIL! · Puzzle #44

ACROSS

2) "I must lose weight, so I will ___ ___ fatty foods."

4) "Let's order a small pizza. On ___ thought, let's order a large pizza. I'm very hungry!"

5) "___ ___ Julio is a doctor, he smokes!"

DOWN

1) "I was ___ ___ meet James at a restaurant last night, but I forgot!"

2) "I was reading a book on the bus, so I forgot to ___ ___ at my stop."

3) "We want to go swimming, but it might rain."
   ▪ "Let's ___ ___ chance and go to the beach anyway."

For answers, see page 368

he **was successful** / he **succeeded** / he **had success**
NOT ~~he success~~; NOT ~~he successful~~

We had a lot of success with the Imax light. Bob was very successful. He succeeded in getting 500 orders.

MORE EXAMPLES 💬

"I'd always wanted to climb Mount Everest and finally I **succeeded**."

"I **had** a lot of **success** with importing. I **was successful** because I worked hard."

309

on average

about; around

This is the result when you add amounts together, then divide by the number of amounts.

MORE EXAMPLES 🗩

"Children watch, **on average**, five hours of television every day."

"I cook chicken, **on average**, once every two months."

For *once every two months*, see page 286

do well

be financially successful

MORE EXAMPLES 🖝

"Two years ago, I didn't **do** very **well**. I made only five sales. But I **did well** last year. I made over 70 sales!"

"Look at Frank's expensive new car! He must be **doing well**."

For *ago*, see page 46
For *must be*, see page 356

the bottom line is

the thing I'm really trying to say is; the main idea is

MORE EXAMPLES 🗨

"I worked hard on the project. I tried my best. But **the bottom line is** I couldn't finish it."

"He's lazy, his work is not good, and he's late every day. **The bottom line is** we have to let him go."

For *let him go*, see page 333

Could you go over that again?

Ask this if you need someone to repeat a lot of information.

MORE EXAMPLES 💬

"**Could you go over** the instructions **again**? I didn't understand everything you said."

A: "... then turn left and then right and then..."

B: "Sorry, I'm not following you. **Could you go over** the directions **again**?"

For *I'm not following you*, see page 36

have a good time

Say this before someone goes
somewhere enjoyable.

MORE EXAMPLES 🗩

A: "Mom, I'm going to my friend's house now."
B: "Okay, **have a good time**."

A: "My sister will be here any minute now.
We're going out for dinner."
B: "**Have a good time**."

For *any minute now*, see page 222

```
                                          ┌─┐
                                          │1│
                    ┌─┐      ┌─┬─┬─┬─┐
                    │2│      │3│ │ │ │
                    ├─┤      └─┴─┴─┴─┤
┌─┬─┬─┬─┬─┬─┬─┬─┬─┐ │ │              │ │
│4│ │ │ │ │ │ │ │ │ │ │              └─┘
└─┴─┴─┴─┤ │ ├─┴─┴─┘ │ │
        │ │ │5│ │ │ │ │
        │ │ └─┴─┴─┴─┘ │
┌─┬─┬─┬─┤ │              
│6│ │ │ │ │ │              
└─┴─┴─┴─┴─┴─┘              
```

ACROSS

3) "My stomach is too big and my pants are too tight. The bottom ___ is I need to lose weight."

4) "Did you do well on your exams?" ▪ "Yes, I was ___ because I studied hard."

5) "Tomorrow I'm going on vacation to Florida!" ▪ "Well, ___ ___ good time."

6) "I didn't understand the instructions. Could you ___ ___ them again?"

DOWN

1) "Our company has many new clients. We are doing ___ this year."

2) "Our students are from 19 to 25 years old. They are, on ___, 22 years old."

For answers, see page 368

hear of something / someone

know that something / someone **exists**

MORE EXAMPLES 🗩

A: "The newspaper says that Sharon Stanley died!"

B: "Who is she? I've never **heard of** her."

A: "Have you seen the movie *Danger Zone*?"

B: "No, but I've **heard of** it. My sister told me about it."

Is something included?

Is the cost of something already added on to the price?

NOT ~~Is it include breakfast?~~

MORE EXAMPLES 🗩

A: "I'm interested in this laptop for $1,999.
   Is the carrying case **included**?"
B: "Yes, you get the laptop and the case, all
   for $1,999."

A: "How much is this watch?"
B: "$100."
A: "**Is** tax **included**?"
B: "No. With tax, it comes to $107."

For *comes to*, see page 334

it depends on something

something **will decide for me**

NOT it's depend

MORE EXAMPLES

A: "How much does it cost to mail a package?"
B: "**It depends on** the weight."

A: "Are you going to buy one shirt or two?"
B: "**It depends on** the price."

on leave

having planned absence from work

MORE EXAMPLES

A: "Does Nancy still work here?"
B: "Yes, but she's **on leave** taking care of her mother."

"My wife is **on** maternity **leave**. We just had a baby, so she has three months off!"

NOTE: on maternity leave = absent from work to give birth

For *have three months off*, see page 325

bring someone up to date

tell someone **the most recent information**

Can you bring me up to date?

Sure. On Monday
Mr. Templeton called you.
He didn't leave a message.
Yesterday Diane Lane
came to see you.
And this morning…

MORE EXAMPLES 🗩

A: "Please **bring** me **up to date** on the computer problem."

B: "I fixed it. Then it broke again. Now it's at the repair shop."

A: "How's Ann? I haven't seen her for years!"

B: "Let me **bring** you **up to date**. She got married, moved to Japan, and now she teaches English."

For *I haven't seen her for*, see page 187

Can you tell me how to get to a place?

This is a polite way to ask for directions.

MORE EXAMPLES 🗨

A: "**Can you tell me how to get to** Whitman's Jewelers?"
B: "Take the elevator to the third floor and turn left."

A: "**Can you tell me how to get to** the human resources department?"
B: "Go down the hall and you'll see it."

GRAB A PENCIL! · Puzzle #46

ACROSS

1) "Let me bring you __ __ __. I got married, had two children, and recently started my own company."

5) "Louis is not working this week. He's on ___. His wife is having a baby."

6) "Can you tell me __ __ __ to the bank?"
   ▪ "Go straight and turn left on Mill Street."

DOWN

2) "Are you going to the party?" ▪ "It __ __ my wife. If she wants to go, we'll go."

3) "I'd like to buy this electronic toy. Are the batteries ___?" ▪ "No, they are sold separately."

4) "Do you know who Mick Jagger is?" ▪ "No, I've never __ __ him. Is he an actor?"

For answers, see page 368

even if it rains

it might rain, but rain is not important —
rain **will not change the situation**

NOT even it rains

MORE EXAMPLES 🗩

"José is a great student. He studies every day. **Even if** he's tired, he studies."

"**Even if** a customer doesn't buy anything, be polite to him or her."

a no-win situation

a situation that can have only bad results

MORE EXAMPLES 🗩

"When a supermarket opened near our store, we lost customers. Now, we can't sell the store. It's **a no-win situation**."

"If I work, I have to pay for a babysitter. If I stop working, I will lose money. It's **a no-win situation**."

have time off

have non-working time arranged by the company

MORE EXAMPLES 🗨

"I **have** a week **off** in July, so I might go to Spain."

A: "Do you work on weekends?"
B: "Only on Saturdays. I **have** Sundays **off**."

get together with someone

meet someone **socially**

MORE EXAMPLES 🍃

"Would you like to **get together** next week? We could go and see a movie."

A: "I'm leaving next week."
B: "Let's **get together** for lunch before you leave."

as for something

Say this to introduce a topic.

NOT ~~about the hotel~~

MORE EXAMPLES 🖅

"Sergio's is a good restaurant. **As for** the service, it's fast and the waiters are friendly. **As for** the price, it's pretty cheap."

A: "What do we need for the party?"
B: "**As for** food, we need a cake. **As for** decorations, let's buy some balloons."

What's someone / something **like?**

Tell me about someone or something.

What's Hawaii like?

ARRIVAL HALL

It's hot and beautiful, and there are lots of mountains, and the people are friendly and...

MORE EXAMPLES 🖎

A: "**What's** that restaurant **like**?"
B: "Well, the food is spicy and it's a little expensive."

A: "**What's** your boss **like**?"
B: "He's very serious. On the other hand, he's very kind."

For *on the other hand*, see page 358

ACROSS
2) "My classes end in May. My job starts in July. I ___ one month ___ in between."
5) "If I walk, I'll be late. If I drive, I won't find a parking space. It's a ___-___ situation."
6) "I love my job. I might win the lottery, but ___ ___ I get rich, I will keep my job."

DOWN
1) "Last night I ___ together with some friends. We went out for dinner."
3) "Let's paint the living room green and the kitchen yellow. ___ ___ the bedrooms, let's use wallpaper."
4) "What's your school ___?" ▪ "It's big and modern, and the teachers are very good."

For answers, see page 368

short for something

a shorter way to say a word

MORE EXAMPLES 🗨

"S'pore is **short for** Singapore."

A: "I need to buy milk and a veggie."
B: "What's a veggie?"
A: "It's **short for** vegetable."

know how

have the skill or knowledge

MORE EXAMPLES 🗩

A: "Do you **know how** to use this fax machine?"

B: "No, but I'll figure it out."

"Mom **knows how** to type, but she doesn't **know how** to use a computer."

For *figure it out*, see page 160

say that / say to

NOT ~~you said me~~; NOT ~~I said him~~

MORE EXAMPLES 🖝

A: "What did you **say to** him?"
B: "I **said that** I was interested in the job."

"She **said that** she has two brothers, and she told me that they're twins."

For *told me*, see page 299

let someone **go**

take away someone's **job**

MORE EXAMPLES 🗩

"He took money from the company, so his boss **let** him **go**."

"Our company isn't doing well. We **let** five people **go** to save some money."

For *do well*, see page 311

it **comes to**

Say this before the total amount.

MORE EXAMPLES 🗨

"I bought a lot of food last week. My bill **came to** $200."

A: "How much is this?"
B: "It's $6. With tax, it **comes to** $6.42."

give me five minutes

Say this when you need someone to wait.

Just give me 5 minutes.
I'm almost ready.

MORE EXAMPLES 🗩

A: "When can you deliver the sofa?"
B: "Can you **give me** a few days? I'm very busy this week."

A: "Which hotel is best?"
B: "I don't know, but if you **give me** 30 minutes, I'll find out."

For *find out*, see page 258

ACROSS
4) "Lucy was late for work every day, so the company ___ her ___. Now she has no job."
5) "What did you say __ Mike?" ▪ "I said ___ we should go to the movies."
6) "Why don't you go skiing with your friends?" ▪ "I don't ___ ___ to ski. I never learned."

DOWN
1) "I can repair your computer, but please ___ me a few days. I'm very busy this week."
2) "Ad is ___ ___ advertisement."
3) "We ordered a lot of food at the restaurant. Our bill ___ ___ $300!"

For answers, see page 368

in case something happens
because something **might happen**

MORE EXAMPLES 🗨

A: "Don't forget to buy eggs."
B: "I'd better write it down **in case** I forget."

A: "Why are you putting a smoke alarm on the wall?"
B: "**In case** there's a fire."

it's up to someone

someone **decides**

MORE EXAMPLES 🗩

A: "What color will you paint your house?"

B: "**It's not up to** me. **It's up to** my wife. She will decide."

A: "Can customers return products?"

B: "**It's up to** the manager. It depends on the situation."

For *it depends on*, see page 318

during something

at the same time as something

during + noun

NOT ~~during we watch the movie~~

MORE EXAMPLES 🗩

"**During the flight**, I read two books."

"We visited friends **during our vacation**."

"**During the meeting**, I fell asleep."

NOTE: noun = thing (book, man, house)

What's taking so long?

Why is something taking a long time?

MORE EXAMPLES 💬

"We've been waiting for the bus for an hour! **What's taking so long?**"

A: "He still hasn't arrived. **What's taking so long?**"
B: "He's stuck in traffic."

For *stuck in traffic*, see page 23

sleep in

wake up later than usual — by choice

I love to sleep in on Sundays.

MORE EXAMPLES ✒

"I can **sleep in** tomorrow morning because I have the day off!"

"I feel great! I **slept in** until 9 o'clock this morning."

For *have the day off*, see page 325

speaking of something

Say this when a word makes
you think of a new topic.

MORE EXAMPLES 🗩

A: "I want to mail this letter."
B: "**Speaking of** mail, did you get a postcard
   from Dave?"

A: "Joe bought a new car."
B: "**Speaking of** cars, I left my bag in your
   car. Did you find it?"

For *left*, see page 232

GRAB A PENCIL! · Puzzle #49

ACROSS
1) "I'm not going to wake up early tomorrow. I'm going to sleep ___."
4) "We ordered our food 30 minutes ago! ___ ___ so long?" ▪ "Maybe they forgot our order."
5) "Can I take the test with a red pen?" ▪ "It's ___ ___ the teacher. You'll have to ask her."

DOWN
1) "When I travel, I always bring medicine in my bag ___ ___ I get sick."
2) "Ted emailed me from Italy." ▪ "___ ___ Italy, let's try that new Italian restaurant."
3) "I learned to swim ___ my vacation."

For answers, see page 368

343

How are you getting
somewhere?

Ask this to find out if someone is going to take a plane, train, car, bus, etc.

MORE EXAMPLES 🖝

A: "**How are you getting** to the conference?"
B: "By taxi."

A: "**How are you getting** home after the party?"
B: "Jane's going to drop me off."

For *drop me off*, see page 72

Could I ask you a favor?

Ask this before requesting someone's help.

MORE EXAMPLES 🗩

"Julio, **could I ask you a favor?** Could help me read this form? It's in Spanish and I can't understand it."

A: "**Could I ask you a favor?**"
B: "Yes?"
A: "Could you give me a hand with these boxes?"

For *give me a hand,* see page 176

How would you like to pay?

**Do you want to pay by cash,
check or credit card?**

MORE EXAMPLES 🗨

A: "Your bill comes to $47.95. **How would
you like to pay?**"
B: "By cash, please."

A: "**How would you like to pay?**"
B: "I'll pay by check."

NOTE: pay **by** cash, check or credit card

For *comes to*, see page 334

There's something wrong with something

Say this when you are not sure
what the problem is.

There's something
wrong with my printer.

MORE EXAMPLES 🗩

"There's something wrong with the air
conditioner. It's making a funny noise."

"There's something wrong with my leg. It
hurts when I walk."

For *funny*, see page 249

how soon

what is the earliest time

MORE EXAMPLES 🗩

A: "**How soon** can you finish the project?"
B: "We can get it done by Friday."

A: "**How soon** can you start working?"
B: "I can start on Monday."

For *get it done*, see page 240
For *by Friday*, see page 117

Can I ask what it's regarding?

Ask this to learn why someone
wants to speak to someone.

MORE EXAMPLES

A: "I'd like to see the manager!"
B: "**Can I ask what it's regarding?**"
A: "I bought a computer here and it's broken."

A: (on the phone) "May I speak to Mr. Yi?"
B: "**Can I ask what it's regarding?**"
A: "It's regarding his account at Union Bank."

ACROSS
4) "Police! Hurry! ___ ___ will you be here?"
   ▪ "We will be there in five minutes."
5) "Can I speak to Ms. Lim?" ▪ "Can I ask what
   it's ___?" ▪ "I'm calling about my bill."
6) "___ ___ you like to pay for this shirt?" ▪ "By
   credit card, please."

DOWN
1) "How are you ___ to the party?" ▪ "I'm going to
   drive."
2) "There's something ___ ___ the refrigerator.
   It's not cold."
3) "Could I ask ___ ___ ___?" ▪ "Sure." ▪ "Could
   you help me move this desk?"

For answers, see page 368

has nothing to do with
someone / something
does not concern or involve
someone / something

MORE EXAMPLES 🗩

A: "Did you quit your job because of the pay?"
B: "No, it **has nothing to do with** pay. I want to start my own company."

A: "Are you angry with me?"
B: "No, I'm angry with Paul. It **has nothing to do with** you."

can't make it

not able to attend

MORE EXAMPLES 🗩

A: "Is Bob coming to the movie?"
B: "No, he's working late. He **can't make it**."

A: "The meeting starts at 3 o'clock sharp."
B: "I **can't make it** by three. I'll be a little late."

For *3 o'clock sharp*, see page 201
For *by three*, see page 117

make sure

confirm; ensure

Make sure she eats her vegetables. And make sure Tommy brushes his teeth. And make sure he...

MORE EXAMPLES 🗩

A: "Please **make sure** we have enough chairs for the meeting."

B: "I've already **made sure**."

"Could you **make sure** you turn off the computer before you leave?"

an hour **late**

NOT ~~late an hour~~

They told us to come at 7 o'clock.

It's 8 o'clock now. We are an hour late.

MORE EXAMPLES 🗩

"I'm stuck in traffic right now. I'll be a few minutes **late**."

"I got to the doctor's office on time, but the doctor was 20 minutes **late**!"

For *stuck in traffic*, see page 23

dressed up

wearing their best clothes

Everyone is dressed up! I thought this was a barbeque!

MORE EXAMPLES 🗩

"My wife likes to get **dressed up**. But I prefer casual clothes."

A: "Why are you so **dressed up**?"
B: "I have a meeting with the president of the company."

must be

Say this when you are 95% sure
about something.

Mr. Lee, this must be your brother.

That's right. This is my brother Alfred.

MORE EXAMPLES 🗩

"I took my shoe to the repair shop a month ago. It **must be** ready by now."

"I just called the store, but no one answered the phone. It **must be** closed."

For *ago,* see page 46

ACROSS

3) "I'm dressed ___ because I'm going to a wedding."

5) "I think I locked the door, but please check and ___ ___ it's locked."

6) "You shouldn't discuss my problem with Ken. My problem has nothing ___ ___ with him."

DOWN

1) "Look! Everyone's clothes are wet! It ___ ___ raining."

2) "He arrived ten minutes after the meeting started. He was ___ minutes ___."

4) "Are you coming to the baseball game on Saturday?" ▪ "Sorry, I can't ___ ___."

For answers, see page 368

on the other hand

Say this before you give an opposite
or contrasting idea.

MORE EXAMPLES 🍷

"Studying medicine is very interesting. **On the other hand**, it's very difficult."

A: "London is a beautiful city."
B: "Yes, but **on the other hand**, it rains a lot."

to tell you the truth

Say this when you want to speak honestly —
often before saying something negative.

> Are you excited
> about the new baby?

> To tell you the
> truth, I'm not excited,
> I'm worried. Babies
> are expensive!

MORE EXAMPLES 🔊

A: "How was my speech?"
B: "Good, but **to tell you the truth**, it was a
   bit too long."

"He's a kind teacher, but **to tell you the
truth**, his class is boring."

put someone in charge
give someone the job of leader or supervisor

MORE EXAMPLES 🗨

"If my husband and I go out, we **put** our oldest son **in charge** at home."

"I **put** Sara **in charge** of the party because she is good at organizing events."

For *good at*, see page 82

keep someone posted

give someone **information when there are new developments**

Has she had the baby yet?

Not yet but I'll keep you posted. I'll call you when something happens.

MORE EXAMPLES 💬

A: "Did the new client sign the contract?"
B: "No, but I'll **keep** you **posted**. I'll call you when he signs."

A: "The workers will start building today."
B: "Please **keep** me **posted** on their progress."

the day before yesterday

Not ~~yesterday before yesterday~~

MORE EXAMPLES 🗨

"I was sick **the day before yesterday**, but yesterday I felt fine."

"It was a 50 hour bus ride! We left **the day before yesterday** and we arrived today."

once a year

NOT ~~one year one time~~

MORE EXAMPLES 🗩

A: "I exercise **once a** week."
B: "Really? I only exercise once every two or
  three weeks."

A: "How often do you check your email?"
B: "**Once a** day."
A: "I check mine twice a day, sometimes
  three times a day."

For *once every*, see page 286

GRAB A PENCIL! · Puzzle #52

ACROSS

2) "Andy is a naughty boy. ___ the other ___, he's very smart."

5) "Today is December 20th, so ___ ___ ___ yesterday was the 18th."

6) "When the boss was away, he ___ me ___ charge of the whole department."

DOWN

1) "How was the restaurant?" ▪ "___ ___ ___ the truth, the food wasn't very good."

3) "I haven't gotten a job yet, but I'll keep you ___. I'll call you when I get a job."

4) "How often do you wash the floors?" ▪ "___ ___ week. I wash them every Monday."

For answers, see page 368

364

ANSWER KEY

PUZZLE 1: ACROSS: 1) jackson, 4) shortof,
5) keepgoing, 6) onhold; DOWN: 2) chargeof, 3) dropby

PUZZLE 2: ACROSS: 1) aheadof, 4) itsfor, 5) ihelpyou;
DOWN: 2) amoveon, 3) for, 5) in

PUZZLE 3: ACROSS: 3) outof, 5) goodtime, 6) heldup;
DOWN: 1) nowonder, 2) upsidedown, 4) tiedup

PUZZLE 4: ACROSS: 2) onme, 4) stuckin, 5) yet;
DOWN: 1) pressure, 2) off, 3) mymind

PUZZLE 5: ACROSS: 4) getthrough, 5) theworld,
6) wasby; DOWN: 1) boat, 2) rightaway, 3) putup

PUZZLE 6: ACROSS: 2) cutoff, 4) secondto, 5) comesin,
6) havechange; DOWN: 1) following, 3) from

PUZZLE 7: ACROSS: 2) ago, 4) like, 6) cheers;
DOWN: 1) makeup, 3) discuss, 5) been

PUZZLE 8: ACROSS: 5) to, 6) sidetracked;
DOWN: 1) oversleep, 2) stayedup, 3) forthe, 4) myway

PUZZLE 9: ACROSS: 2) winwin, 5) it, 6) getit;
DOWN: 1) pickup, 3) inthe, 4) about

PUZZLE 10: ACROSS: 1) off, 2) mindif, 3) check,
4) puton; DOWN: 1) ofthat, 2) mean

PUZZLE 11: ACROSS: 4) up 5) thedayafter, 6) chipin;
DOWN: 1) dropoff, 2) between, 3) have

PUZZLE 12: ACROSS: 5) sogood, 6) taketurns;
DOWN: 1) goodat, 2) longas, 3) upwith, 4) remind

PUZZLE 13: ACROSS: 1) despite, 3) whereis, 5) notto,
6) asa; DOWN: 2) sorryto, 4) sounds

PUZZLE 14: ACROSS: 3) from, 5) steppedout, 6) ingood; DOWN: 1) good, 2) adelay, 4) putyou

PUZZLE 15: ACROSS: 2) to, 3) back, 5) really, 6) grapevine; DOWN: 1) toobad, 4) charge

PUZZLE 16: ACROSS: 4) secondfrom, 6) ahead; DOWN: 1) inagood, 2) they, 3) off, 5) on

PUZZLE 17: ACROSS: 2) apart, 5) by, 6) raninto; DOWN: 1) whatabout, 3) thisis, 4) work

PUZZLE 18: ACROSS: 2) what, 4) eyetoeye, 6) for; DOWN: 1) madeof, 3) itin, 5) worth

PUZZLE 19: ACROSS: 3) ridof, 4) thebankis, 6) made; DOWN: 1) shoot, 2) lookup, 5) have

PUZZLE 20: ACROSS: 2) take, 3) muchlonger, 4) soldout, 5) mindgoing; DOWN: 1) waythrough, 3) mention

PUZZLE 21: ACROSS: 4) doublecheck, 5) might, 6) inthat; DOWN: 1) connection, 2) matter, 3) held

PUZZLE 22: ACROSS: 3) see, 4) inthose, 5) get; DOWN: 1) byear, 2) istaken, 3) setup

PUZZLE 23: ACROSS: 5) havingwith, 6) ride; DOWN: 1) byfar, 2) positive, 3) outhow, 4) tipof

PUZZLE 24: ACROSS: 1) off, 5) thathe, 6) doesn't; DOWN: 2) fortune, 3) atthe, 4) onatin

PUZZLE 25: ACROSS: 5) insteadof, 6) run; DOWN: 1) comewith, 2) inwriting, 3) throwaway, 4) itover

PUZZLE 26: ACROSS: 3) bringup, 5) hand, 6) for; DOWN: 1) enough, 2) withme, 4) readyto

PUZZLE 27: ACROSS: 1) seenfor, 4) left, 5) outof; DOWN: 1) split, 2) other, 3) upto

PUZZLE 28: ACROSS: 1) returning, 4) get, 5) back;
DOWN: 1) regards, 2) through, 3) intouch

PUZZLE 29: ACROSS: 2) sharp, 3) all, 5) meknow,
6) theright; DOWN: 1) thenext, 4) line

PUZZLE 30: ACROSS: 3) in, 4) turn, 5) moveon,
6) hangup; DOWN: 1) feetlong, 2) didgo

PUZZLE 31: ACROSS: 1) down, 5) nopoint, 6) makea;
DOWN: 2) wrapped, 3) being, 4) in

PUZZLE 32: ACROSS: 1) point, 4) afford, 5) strings;
DOWN: 2) theas, 3) worth, 4) any

PUZZLE 33: ACROSS: 2) out, 4) within, 6) goover;
DOWN: 1) coming, 3) lendyou, 5) for

PUZZLE 34: ACROSS: 1) wordwith, 5) arow, 6) pickup;
DOWN: 2) outof, 3) insick, 4) leave

PUZZLE 35: ACROSS: 1) last, 4) expected, 5) humor;
DOWN: 1) last, 2) get, 3) getout

PUZZLE 36: ACROSS: 1) funny, 5) tohear, 6) doaboutit;
DOWN: 2) nowon, 3) preferto, 4) letgo

PUZZLE 37: ACROSS: 3) reach, 4) into, 5) get 6) wouldit;
DOWN: 1) takeget, 2) findout

PUZZLE 38: ACROSS: 1) havebeen, 3) have,
5) doesmean, 6) back; DOWN: 2) awayon, 4) theway

PUZZLE 39: ACROSS: 1) atleast, 3) beenlong, 5) togo;
DOWN: 2) shortby, 3) beall, 4) looks

PUZZLE 40: ACROSS: 4) backto, 5) showedaround,
6) faras; DOWN: 1) yourselfat, 2) howwas, 3) standsfor

PUZZLE 41: ACROSS: 3) handson, 4) helpyourself,
6) upwith; DOWN: 1) notice, 2) backforth, 5) every

PUZZLE 42: ACROSS: 1) recommend, 5) press, 6) had; DOWN: 2) offhand, 3) moveup, 4) getby

PUZZLE 43: ACROSS: 3) difficultto, 5) thebest, 6) afternext; DOWN: 1) told, 2) words, 4) iwere

PUZZLE 44: ACROSS: 2) giveup, 4) second, 5) eventhough; DOWN: 1) supposedto, 2) getoff, 3) takea

PUZZLE 45: ACROSS: 3) line, 4) successful, 5) havea, 6) goover; DOWN: 1) well, 2) average

PUZZLE 46: ACROSS: 1) uptodate, 5) leave, 6) howtoget; DOWN: 2) dependson, 3) included, 4) heardof

PUZZLE 47: ACROSS: 2) haveoff, 5) nowin, 6) evenif; DOWN: 1) got, 3) asfor, 4) like

PUZZLE 48: ACROSS: 4) letgo, 5) tothat, 6) knowhow; DOWN: 1) give, 2) shortfor, 3) cameto

PUZZLE 49: ACROSS: 1) in, 4) whatstaking, 5) upto; DOWN: 1) incase, 2) speakingof, 3) during

PUZZLE 50: ACROSS: 4) howsoon, 5) regarding, 6) howwould; DOWN: 1) getting, 2) wrongwith, 3) youafavor

PUZZLE 51: ACROSS: 3) up, 5) makesure, 6) todo; DOWN: 1) mustbe, 2) tenlate, 4) makeit

PUZZLE 52: ACROSS: 2) onhand, 5) thedaybefore, 6) putin; DOWN: 1) totellyou, 3) posted, 4) oncea

LANGUAGE SUCCESS PRESS

ORDER FORM

TITLE	Quantity	Line Total
Say it Better in English...$24.95		
Lose Your Accent in 28 Days (Complete System with Workbook, CD-ROM, Audio CD)...$49.95		
Speak Business English Like an American (select language version) ☐ for Native Speakers of Any Language ☐ for Russian Speakers ☐ for Chinese Speakers (Book & Audio CD)...$29.95		
Speak English Like an American (select language version): ☐ for Native Speakers of Any Language ☐ for Chinese Speakers ☐ for Russian Speakers ☐ for Spanish Speakers ☐ for Japanese Speakers (Book & Audio CD)...$24.95		
Inglés ¡Qué buen acento!: An English Pronunciation Guide for Spanish Speakers (Book & 2 Audio CDs)...$29.95		
Subtotal		
Shipment to Michigan Add 6% Sales Tax		
Shipping (see below)		
TOTAL		

U.S. Shipping: $4.95 for orders up to $50. $6.95 for orders from $50.01 to $75. $8.95 for orders $75.01-$100. $11.95 for orders from $100.01-$200. Add an additional $4 for each additional $100 or part thereof. **International Shipping**: Multiply the U.S. shipping rate by 2.

Please charge my: ☐ VISA ☐ MASTERCARD ☐ AMERICAN EXPRESS

Card #_____Expiration_____

Name on card_____

Ship to:

Name_____

Organization_____

Address_____

City_____ State_____ Zip_____ Country _____

Phone_____ E-mail_____

📄 FAX this form to Language Success Press: 1-303-484-2004
✉ MAIL this form to: Language Success Press ♦ 2232 S. Main St #345 ♦ Ann Arbor, MI 48103
☎ CALL Toll-Free to order (24 hours a day, 7 days a week): 1-866-577-7323
🖰 ORDER ONLINE: www.languagesuccesspress.com